COMPUTER SCIENCE, TECHNOLOGY AND APPLICATIONS

DATA SECURITY, DATA MINING AND DATA MANAGEMENT

TECHNOLOGIES AND CHALLENGES

COMPUTER SCIENCE, TECHNOLOGY AND APPLICATIONS

Additional books in this series can be found on Nova's website under the Series tab.

Additional e-books in this series can be found on Nova's website under the e-book tab.

COMPUTER SCIENCE, TECHNOLOGY AND APPLICATIONS

DATA SECURITY, DATA MINING AND DATA MANAGEMENT TECHNOLOGIES AND CHALLENGES

SERGE O'BYRNE
EDITOR

New York

Copyright © 2013 by Nova Science Publishers, Inc.

All rights reserved. No part of this book may be reproduced, stored in a retrieval system or transmitted in any form or by any means: electronic, electrostatic, magnetic, tape, mechanical photocopying, recording or otherwise without the written permission of the Publisher.

For permission to use material from this book please contact us:
Telephone 631-231-7269; Fax 631-231-8175
Web Site: http://www.novapublishers.com

NOTICE TO THE READER

The Publisher has taken reasonable care in the preparation of this book, but makes no expressed or implied warranty of any kind and assumes no responsibility for any errors or omissions. No liability is assumed for incidental or consequential damages in connection with or arising out of information contained in this book. The Publisher shall not be liable for any special, consequential, or exemplary damages resulting, in whole or in part, from the readers' use of, or reliance upon, this material. Any parts of this book based on government reports are so indicated and copyright is claimed for those parts to the extent applicable to compilations of such works.

Independent verification should be sought for any data, advice or recommendations contained in this book. In addition, no responsibility is assumed by the publisher for any injury and/or damage to persons or property arising from any methods, products, instructions, ideas or otherwise contained in this publication.

This publication is designed to provide accurate and authoritative information with regard to the subject matter covered herein. It is sold with the clear understanding that the Publisher is not engaged in rendering legal or any other professional services. If legal or any other expert assistance is required, the services of a competent person should be sought. FROM A DECLARATION OF PARTICIPANTS JOINTLY ADOPTED BY A COMMITTEE OF THE AMERICAN BAR ASSOCIATION AND A COMMITTEE OF PUBLISHERS.

Additional color graphics may be available in the e-book version of this book.

Library of Congress Cataloging-in-Publication Data

ISBN: 978-1-62417-582-4

Published by Nova Science Publishers, Inc. † New York

CONTENTS

Preface vii

Chapter 1 Clustering Algorithms in Radiobiology
and DNA Damage Quantification 1
Ziad Francis and Agnieszka Stypczynska

Chapter 2 Data Mining for Genomic Information 31
P. D. Freitas and C. A. Santos

Chapter 3 Data Management in the Semantic Web 49
Lubos Matejicek

Chapter 4 Nothing Happens until It Happens 67
Mads Ronald Dahl and Eivind Ortind Simonsen

Index 75

PREFACE

In this book, the authors discuss the new technologies and challenges of data security, data mining and data management. Topics include clustering algorithms in radiobiology and DNA damage quantification; data mining for searching genomic information; data management in the semantic web; and how fragile data security can be when the system architecture, authorization and validation is founded on a personal identification number (PIN).

Chapter 1 – Ionizing particles effect on living cells has been a hot topic in recent research activities where applications are of interest for radioprotection, radiobiology and radiotherapy fields. The radio-induced DNA damage is considered to be the most lethal effect of radiation on living cells. In fact, ionizing particles can interact with the DNA of a cell and the resulting modifications can lead to severe damages that the cell is unable to repair. It is also possible that mutation caused by a missed repair can have consequences leading to cell death or to carcinogenesis.

Using the Monte-Carlo method it is possible to simulate the track of a particle crossing a target volume, taking into account its interactions with the medium molecules and revealing the positions and the amount of the energy deposition at each interaction point. Several methods of analysis are then published in order to estimate the final effect of such a track on the cell and the cell survival probability. One way to study this is to look into the yields of energy deposition clusters that can lead to clustered DNA damages also called complex lesions which are lethal for the cell.

Although the Hartigan K-Means algorithm was previously used in the literature to compare energy deposition clustering of different types of radiation, there have been no other efforts of using different algorithms in this field. Here in this study, a brief review summarizes the so far obtained results showing the capacities and the limits of K-Means for this kind of applications and then an adapted version of the Density Based Spatial Clustering Algorithm with Noise (DBSCAN) method is presented with application to protons and ions induced DNA damage.

As for many of the clustering algorithms the main issue of such type of analysis remains the computing time and power that are required to treat and analyze the presented database. A summary of the performance of DBSCAN is presented with respect to the actual size of data that is treated in radiobiology and DNA damage applications.

Chapter 2 – Data mining is an approach used for Knowledge Discovery in Databases (KDD), which is responsible for detecting new and relevant relationships in large amounts of stored data through the development of pattern recognition technologies using statistical and mathematical tools. This method is fast and efficient and is not a particularly recent approach, and it is applicable to statistics, economics, engineering, disease studies in medicine, and other fields. The data are stored electronically, and the search is computerized. Although data mining is still evolving, many areas of study are already using this important resource. In molecular biology, for example, the discovery of molecular markers, such as microsatellites (simple sequence repeats, or SSRs) and single nucleotide polymorphisms (SNPs) using this approach has increased over the last decade in several organisms, such as plants, clams, shrimp and humans. These markers are even more useful when located in expressed regions of the genome, which are known as expressed sequence tags (ESTs). Characterizing EST-SSRs and EST-SNPs that may be applicable to genetic studies of economically relevant and threatened species is a useful tool for polymorphism analysis, genetic mapping and quantitative trait loci (QTL) identification.

To identify these markers, owning an EST database (DB) that is capable of data mining is essential. Bioinformatics software eliminates redundancies within each file, and the information generated can be analyzed and regrouped. The ESTs are later submitted to an online DB to search for similarities between the studied sequence (query) and the sequences available online (subject) to elucidate the protein codified by each gene. In shrimp, for example, several highly relevant gene products for homeostasis are highlighted, such as transcription regulatory units and enzyme inhibitors, which links these gene variations, causing different biological responses to stress to EST-SSRs. Data from genomic annotation makes it possible to elucidate a metabolic network, and uniting the fields of genetics and biochemistry to clarify major changes that may be occurring at the cellular level in addition to connecting genotypes to phenotypes. These markers may also be used as biosensors to show particular adaptations to each environment more precisely.

Chapter 3 – Data management encompasses a number of professions that are generally focused on the development, execution and supervision of plans, policies, programs and practices that control, protect, deliver and enhance the value of data and information assets. In the framework of this delineation, Geographic Information Systems (GISs) together with cloud computing represent an emerging computing paradigm, which offers delivering a variety of computing services in a way that has not been experienced previously. In order to develop advanced data management, standard systems must be adapted to more powerful and efficient computing tools. A few examples are used to demonstrate a new way of data management using GIS and cloud computing tools. The examples are dealing with processing of satellite images and aerial photographs that are complemented by spatial objects linked tothe geodatabase. The attached examples also demonstrate the use of cloud-computing tools for data management and semantic web services. It can support decision-making processes in the areas of interest, and indicate potential solutions for other research fields of study. Data management using cloud computing and GIS represents a new application domain that outlines new means in research, and new trends in education. It promises to provide opportunities for delivering a variety of advanced computing services focused on data management. Besides GIS data management, the chapter also describes basic spatial data formats, spatial web basedservices, and new developments based on the geodatabase and its data models. Sharing spatial and temporal data via Internet includes description of the web based services for spatial data management based on the Open Geospatial Consortium (OGC) standards implemented, as examples, inthe Map Server and in the ArcGIS server.

Chapter 4 - Usage of information technology and communication (ICT) is of fundamental importance to the daily operation of the modern organization.

Data security is a chimera in many forms and the on-going production, sharing and storage of knowledge, information and big data have to be robust to withstand the constant development of the digital environment and architecture. Information technology (IT) is used to control and distribute general information, personal data, and highly classified and sensitive data. As part of the university development, the authors have implemented several learning management systems (LMS) used by the administration, teachers, and students. The LMS has become a central part of the university ICT portfolio and provide the opportunities for effective and flexible teaching and learning environments. One set of challenges is to guide and educate the users of the systems in general data security issues, on one side, and keep the system aligned to security standards on the system administration side. These two stakeholders have completely different views and expectations to the system and they operate either frontend (users) or backend (system administration). Thus, a potential misinterpretation of needs can lead to a breach in data security. Furthermore, the organization, IT policy, and standards need more than text, intentions, and publication: it must be pushed and supported to achieve awareness of increased data security.

Digital identification and authentication often relay on unique usernames and passwords. In Denmark every citizen has a unique personal identification number (CPR-number) used for any communication with public services, such as local and national government, education, healthcare, etc. Also, the ID is being used for identification in the private sector, such as banking, renting, and memberships. This widespread usage of the CPR-number makes it the single most important number to any individual.

In this paper the authors will illustrate how fragile data security can be when the system architecture, authorization, and validation are founded on a personal identification number (PIN). The authors tested the automated support systems, where requests for forgotten passwords and account reset options were possible. These systems are often services, such as mail account, cloud computers, LMS, or intranet elements. Since the user identification for these systems could be based on the unique CPR number, chances are that this information can be extracted. In conclusion, the authors urge not to use CPR, social security number, and comparable numbers as identification key for general systems. These numbers are personal and should only be used for registration in administration system with no public access and the highest standard of data security.

In: Data Security, Data Mining ...
Editor: Serge O'Byrne

ISBN: 978-1-62417-582-4
© 2013 Nova Science Publishers, Inc.

Chapter 1

CLUSTERING ALGORITHMS IN RADIOBIOLOGY AND DNA DAMAGE QUANTIFICATION

Ziad Francis[1,2]* and Agnieszka Stypczynska[2#]

[1]Université Saint Joseph, Beirut, Lebanon
[2]The Open University, Milton Keynes, United Kingdom

ABSTRACT

Ionizing particles effect on living cells has been a hot topic in recent research activities where applications are of interest for radioprotection, radiobiology and radiotherapy fields. The radio-induced DNA damage is considered to be the most lethal effect of radiation on living cells. In fact, ionizing particles can interact with the DNA of a cell and the resulting modifications can lead to severe damages that the cell is unable to repair. It is also possible that mutation caused by a missed repair can have consequences leading to cell death or to carcinogenesis.

Using the Monte-Carlo method it is possible to simulate the track of a particle crossing a target volume, taking into account its interactions with the medium molecules and revealing the positions and the amount of the energy deposition at each interaction point. Several methods of analysis are then published in order to estimate the final effect of such a

---

*Université Saint Joseph, Faculty of Sciences, Department of Physics, Mkalles, Beirut, Lebanon.
#The Open University, Faculty of Science, Department of Physical Sciences, Walton Hall, MK7 6AA, Milton Keynes, United Kingdom. E-mail: Ziad.francis@gmail.com.

track on the cell and the cell survival probability. One way to study this is to look into the yields of energy deposition clusters that can lead to clustered DNA damages also called complex lesions which are lethal for the cell.

Although the Hartigan K-Means algorithm was previously used in the literature to compare energy deposition clustering of different types of radiation, there have been no other efforts of using different algorithms in this field. Here in this study, a brief review summarizes the so far obtained results showing the capacities and the limits of K-Means for this kind of applications and then an adapted version of the Density Based Spatial Clustering Algorithm with Noise (DBSCAN) method is presented with application to protons and ions induced DNA damage.

As for many of the clustering algorithms the main issue of such type of analysis remains the computing time and power that are required to treat and analyze the presented database. A summary of the performance of DBSCAN is presented with respect to the actual size of data that is treated in radiobiology and DNA damage applications.

1. INTRODUCTION

Radiation interaction with matter is becoming a hot topic nowadays in many fields, especially in radiobiology. In fact, ionizing particles interaction with biological organisms is of interest for the medical field, cancer treatments using radiotherapy and also for space science and space radioprotection. When an energetic particle goes through biological tissue it can induce excitations, ionizations and molecule modifications in the medium. The most critical modifications are considered to take place in the deoxyribonucleic acid (DNA) since this molecule dictates the cells functioning and any modification can alter the cell cycle and lead to its death. When DNA damage is detected repair processes are triggered within the cell, however the effectiveness of these processes depends largely on the damage type and on the complexity of the damage pattern. So repair might be successful or in some cases might lead to repair induced mutations. This particular aspect is of interest for radiotherapy where one can induce a secondary cancer caused by radio-induced mutations issued from the primary treatment, and also for space radioprotection concerning astronauts going through intense fields of space radiation where the mutation yields probability can be an index for the severity of damages induced during a space mission.

Since the radio induced damage is tightly related to the energy deposition in the medium, a good approximation is used nowadays for therapeutic cases considering that the cell death rate is related to the energy delivered to the medium according to the linear quadratic model thoroughly analyzed by Brenner [1]. As simple as it might look, this model had been in use for many years in the medical field for treatment planning with relatively good results especially for X-rays and electrons irradiations. However, this is more to be considered as an empirical model that was built based on cell survival observations after irradiations. So it does not give any information on what happens inside of the cell or inside of the nucleus, nor does it give any information about cell repair activities or resulting DNA mutations. Moreover, the model predictions can be limited to relatively short term cellular reactions since its parameters are adjusted to cell death within a certain time frame after irradiation. Here it is important to note that effects of radiation on human body can be revealed up to several years after the irradiation phase. The only way to quantify precisely the radiation effect on a biological tissue and predict the resulting reactions is to understand in detail, what happens on the DNA level during irradiation and during the repair phase. Studies in this field are divided into several themes like experiments and theory on microdosimetry, experiments on irradiated DNA analysis techniques and numerical modeling of particles interaction with biological medium.

Since classic dosimetry was not sufficient to analyze particle tracks and energy deposits on the micrometric and the nanometric scale, the microdosimetry formalism was introduced in the 1960s by Harald Rossi and detailed again by Kellerer and Chmelevsky [2, 3]. In the newly introduced concepts the "imparted energy" refers to the particle energy loss within the micrometric volume target and it varies from one particle to another so it is considered a stochastic variable. The "specific energy" is the imparted energy per mass unit and is generally noted by the letter "z", it is the analogue of the absorbed dose in classic dosimetry. The lineal energy transfer represents the imparted energy in a target divided by the mean cord length of the tracks crossing the target volume. The lineal energy is the analog of the linear energy transfer in classic dosimetry. The specific energy and the lineal energy transfer are stochastic quantities and their distributions can be of importance for radiation quality assessment.

Experiments trying to measure specific and lineal energies were carried out by Borak et al. [4] using the so called Tissue Equivalent Proportional Counters (TEPC) and a position-sensitive silicon spectrometer. The underlying idea is to simulate the presence of a tissue micrometric volume using a low pressure equivalent gas. This assumption considers that the energy loss of an energetic particle would be the same through both targets. In this experiment the simulated target was a sphere of 1 µm of diameter irradiated with protons of different kinetic energies. Ionizations induced within the target sphere enable the measurement of the energy imparted to target molecules and consequently the lineal energy can be calculated knowing the target dimensions.

In parallel, many simulation codes were developed in the field, enabling users to simulate the track structure of ionizing particles through sufficiently small targets reaching the sub-micrometer precision. We may site the Geant4-DNA [5] processes of the Geant4 [6, 7] toolkit, where it is possible to simulate protons, electrons, alpha particles and some heavier ions like carbon and iron ions through water targets. In general water is used as an approximation for biological tissue since it is the major component of a living organism and interaction cross sections calculations are relatively simpler for water than for biocompounds. As a more precise approach some codes included DNA bases cross sections instead of water approximation e.g., the PARTRAC code [8-10] where the DNA geometry was modeled on an atomic level building a double helix configuration in a condensed pattern to form a complete fibroblast (and a lymphocyte in a second simulation) chromosome model.

In fact, in whatever methodology that is used, most of the damage calculation relies on analyzing the positions of the damage inducing energy deposit points. For example, since DNA is formed by a double helix meaning having two strands, a double strand break (DSB) is formed when two single strand breaks (SSBs) are located within a certain distance limit from each other. This DNA structure is detailed in the next section, here we are only highlighting the importance of the spatial distribution of energy deposits in defining the density of the created damages. The damage type and density will have an impact on the repair processes effectiveness. As a matter of fact repair processes are triggered within the cell nucleus after irradiation assuming that SSB can be repaired. DSBs are more difficult to repair and the so called complex damages formed by more than 2 SSBs within a relatively small distance are the most challenging for repair activities. Depending on the circumstances a repair process might be successful or can lead to a bad repair meaning mutation one of the causes of long term cancer or even cell death.

Assuming that the spatial distribution of damages is related to the distribution of energy deposits induced by the particle track other methods of simulations were developed assigning to each particle a set of parameters directly related to its track pattern and defining its biological effectiveness [11, 12]. The previously introduced detailed atomic level simulations offer a high precision and relatively accurate description of the events, however they are very time consuming when comes to practical issues. This kind of calculations is often run on complex computing clusters due to lengthy computing time. Other kinds of approaches were explored in order to simplify DNA damage simulations, mostly using statistical approaches [12] or even data mining clustering algorithms [13]. This type of methods discards the detailed geometrical configuration of DNA relying on approximate statistical analysis and leading to relatively good results.

In what follows, we will introduce the DNA molecule structure showing the different properties that are to be taken into account in the simulations, we will also describe briefly the Monte-Carlo track structure simulations and the data mining methods that were used to analyze radiation quality concentrating more on the Density Based Spatial Clustering Applications with Noise (DBSCAN) algorithm [14] and its application in radiobiology applications. Finally, a GPU based programming application will be introduced showing the advantages of such an approach for time acceleration.

2. STRUCTURE OF THE DEOXYRIBONUCLEIC ACID (DNA)

DNA is the heredity polymer material, which has the ability to store and transfer genetic information from parents to descendants. For both, prokaryotic and eukaryotic organisms the information carried by DNA has the significance of providing proper cell functioning and reproduction. The importance of DNA was not clearly understood until the discovery of its double helix structure in the 1950s [15]. James Watson and Francis Crick showed that the DNA structure has two helical chains each coiled round the same axis. Both chains follow the right-handed helices, which run in opposite directions. Moreover, the chains are made of two groups of nitrogenous bases as presented in Figure 1, covalently connected with the backbone consisting of deoxyribose and phosphate group.

The bases are derived from two classes of molecules - purines and pyrimidines presented in Figure 1. In this chapter we will refer to the bases by their names as adenine, guanine, thymine, cytosine and uracil. Bases are linked together in a complementary way via hydrogen bonds, where adenine always bonds with thymine and guanine with cytosine. In the case of ribonucleic acid (RNA) thymine is replaced by uracil (U). Watson and Crick suggested that hydrogen linkages stabilize the whole structure of double helix as shown by Erwin Chargaff [16]. The sequence of bases on a single strand is not restricted in any way but it is known that if the sequence of bases on one strand is given then the complementary combination on the other chain is automatically designated. Figure 2 shows a scheme of base pairing in double helix, where A:T is linked by two hydrogen bonds in contrast to three bonds in G:C [17].

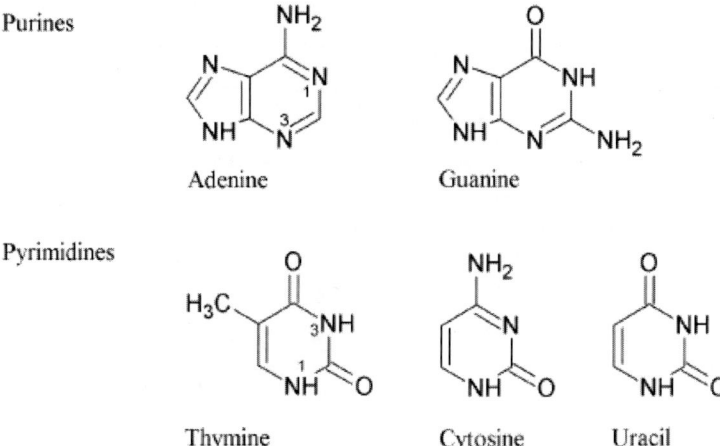

Figure 1. Five nitrogenous bases of DNA and RNA - purines and pyrimidines.

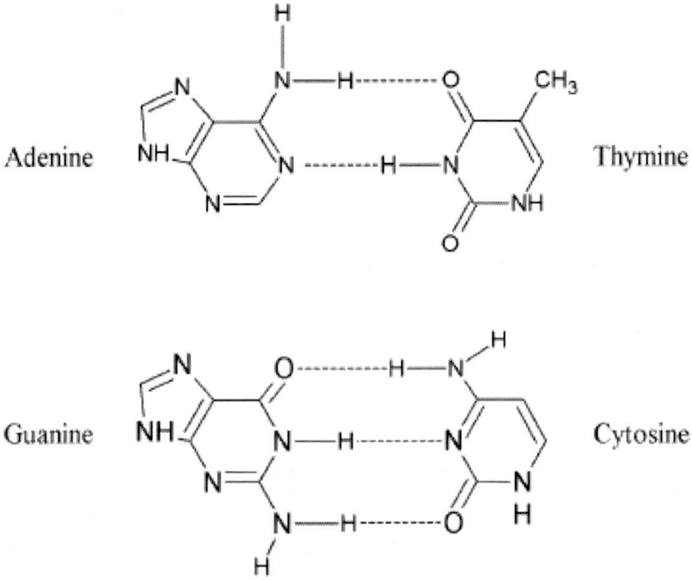

Figure 2. Base pairing in DNA double chain.

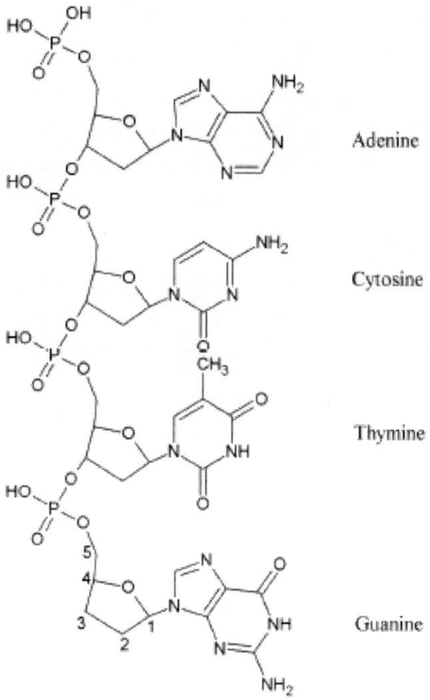

Figure 3. Linkage between nucleobases, sugar and phosphate group.

Long linear repetitions of these dyads (a pair of complementary nucleobases) form the genetic code, which is the information storage and transmission system. The combination of bases within a gene is subdivided into linear non-overlapping triplets. Thus each base triple defines a particular amino acid, for instance, AUG is characteristic for methionine and UGG is the code for tryptophan. Therefore any modification to sequence coded forms may lead to rupture.

Pentose DNA sugar, deoxyribose, is attached to a nucleobase via the glycosidic bond and this structure is called a nucleoside. Furthermore, complexes of DNA base, sugar and phosphate group are known as nucleotides (nucleoside combined with phosphate). Each nucleotide is bonded to its neighbor in the chain by phosphodiester bonds. DNA is made up of a series of nucleotides as shown in Figure 3.

Human DNA and most DNA in eukaryotic cells are tightly bound with proteins called histones. There are five types of histone proteins, which are rich in positively charged basic amino acids and united with the negatively charged phosphate groups in DNA. Histones are also components of chromatin. They act as a spool around which DNA winds, without histones the unwound DNA in chromosomes would be very long. This winding allows the compaction necessary to fit the large genomes of eukaryotes inside cell nuclei. We assume that any other detail on the DNA structure would be out of the scope of this chapter that is why further information can be found in [18].

During irradiation, depending on the ionization position molecule bonds can be modified leading to a break between components of the DNA. Ionizing radiation may directly interact with a DNA molecule leading to the ionization of DNA subunits, this process is characterized as direct damage.

However, in its cellular environment DNA is always hydrated by water molecules and surrounded by proteins. Hence, the incident radiation can create free radicals (highly reactive molecules with unpaired electrons), which cause lesions such as breaks of DNA backbone, base modifications or base removal. Since DNA damage might be induced by secondary species, this type of damage is known as the radiation indirect action [19].

Water is the major constituent of biological systems composing 70% of the mass of the human cell [20] and is necessary for transporting, dissolving, replenishing nutrient and organic matter, as well as for carrying away waste material. Consequently, the direct action of irradiation on the water molecule triggers the formation of hydrated electrons in the form of very strong acid (e_{aq}^-) and the water radical cation ($H_2O^{\cdot+}$), which rapidly loses a proton in the interaction with other water molecule to give the hydroxyl radical. Hydrated electrons decay slowly, lasting a few microseconds and they contribute to the formation of radicals [20]. Ionizing radiation may also directly excite water molecules followed by homolysis (dissociation of the molecule generating two free radicals) into $H^{\cdot}$ and the hydroxyl radical ($OH^{\cdot}$). Oxidizers and reducers such as $OH^{\cdot}$ and $H^{\cdot}$ cause reactions, which may create new molecules. Indeed, it should be emphasized that hydroxyl radical is usually treated as the major active form of oxygen responsible for oxidative damage to DNA. Irradiation of water may also lead to the production of hydrogen and hydrogen peroxide. That is why malignant tissues reveal enlarged concentrations of H_2O_2. The main interactions can be summarized by the following equations:

$$H_2O \xrightarrow{h\nu} H_2O^{\cdot+} + e_{aq}^- \tag{1}$$

$$H_2O^{\cdot+} + H_2O \xrightarrow{fast} H_3O^+ + OH^{\cdot} \tag{2}$$

$$e^-_{aq} \xrightarrow{slow} H^{\cdot} + OH^- \qquad (3)$$

$$H_2O \xrightarrow{hv} H_2O^* \rightarrow H^{\cdot} + OH^{\cdot} \qquad (4)$$

$$H^{\cdot} + H^{\cdot} \rightarrow H_2 \qquad (5)$$

$$e^-_{aq} + e^-_{aq} \rightarrow H_2 + 2OH^- \qquad (6)$$

$$OH^{\cdot} + OH^{\cdot} \rightarrow H_2O_2 \qquad (7)$$

The damages of the DNA can be characterized by single and double strand breaks, base damage and locally multiply damaged sites. Ionizing radiation can result in structural and chemical modifications of double-stranded DNA. As schematically presented in Figure 4 various types of damage to sugar-phosphate backbone of DNA can be quantified into either single strand breaks (SSBs) or/and double strand breaks (DSBs). More precisely, SSBs occur when a single chain in DNA is ruptured. DSBs are characteristic of both strands of the helix being broken within a few base pairs of one another. DSBs can also be formed from metabolic errors, environmental actions (e.g., radicals' reaction) and meiotic recombination (genetic recombination, where sequences of nucleotide are exchanged between two similar DNA molecules). SSBs can be repaired with a relative ease because the complementary nucleotide remains intact and play a role in fixing a defective strand. The repair of DSBs is more challenging because inappropriate repair leads to mutation. There are also other types of DNA break such as base damage and the formation of apyrimidinic/apurinic (AP) site, which can transform into SSBs.

So depending on the damage type we can consider that a successful repair probability decreases with damage complexity. Practically, the so called complex damages are mostly caused by clustered energy depositions induced by ionizing particles, since the damage complexity is dependent from the energy depositions concentration and spatial distribution.

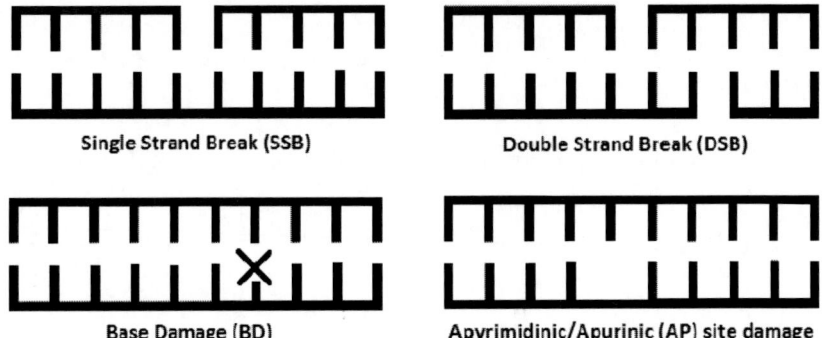

Figure 4. Schematic representation of DNA damages; single and double strand breaks, base damages and the apyrimidinic/apurinic sites damage, for more details see reference [19].

Both SSBs and DSBs can be identified and quantified using experimental techniques like the gel electrophoresis technique as the detection method. The principle of electrophoresis is based on the electromotive force, which moves molecules through a matrix of agarose or polyacrylamide gel under the influence of an electrical field.

The basic damage mechanisms to DNA and other biomacromolecules within the cell and their detection methods have recently been brought into question by the new studies of plasma [21] and X-ray photon [22] interactions with molecules of biological significance. Agarose gel electrophoresis was used by Stypczynska et al. [23] to describe the results of cold plasma irradiation of two DNA/amino acids complexes (using arginine and glycine) in aqueous solution and compare with damage induced by plasma irradiation of pure DNA samples prepared under the same conditions. The results of such work on model of DNA-protein complexes give a basic knowledge and understanding the underlying mechanisms of radiation induced DNA damage and also allow the correlation between the effect of a plasma jet and the damage induced at a molecular level to be explored. X-ray Photoelectron Spectroscopy (XPS) [24-26] is also one of the most common analytical characterization methods, which can provide a detailed knowledge on both the chemical surface composition and the chemical state of the atoms on the surface. XPS has been used to analyze a wide variety of samples including rocks, polymers, powders, fibers and biological specimens. Previous studies recorded with XPS apparatus have revealed that DNA molecule and its constituents are vulnerable upon X-ray and plasma exposure and undergo chemical and structural modifications including loss of supercoiled (SC) form of DNA, base damage, formation of single and double strand breaks.

3. MODELING THE PHYSICAL INTERACTIONS

As already mentioned, understanding the cell reaction to radiation requires a certain details level and knowledge of some processes occurring inside of the cell nucleus during irradiation. In spite of the experimental efforts nowadays it is still impossible to achieve such a molecular resolution in dose measurement and energy deposit analysis especially in biological medium. However, in some experiments by Nardo et al. and by Grosswendt et al., measurements were achieved within few nanometers resolution for alpha particles nanodosimetry analysis [27-30]. This type of experiments reveals somehow the spatial distribution of energy deposit points after the particle's interaction with low pressure propane gas simulating a nanometrical volume. So clusters distributions and clusters of energy deposits can be obtained which is very basic and crucial information about the radiation beam characteristics. Nevertheless, this type of experiments is not easy to realize and mostly not accessible, an alternative would be to use numerical track structure simulation in order to generate particle tracks through sub-cellular volumes. Of course here, we do not mean replacing the experiment by complex numerical operations, but these two approaches are considered as complementary since anyway we still need experimental results to validate the calculations.

It is important to note here that general purpose Monte-Carlo codes such as Geant4 (Geometry and Tracking, see Agostinelli et al. [6]), MCNP (Monte Carlo N-Particle transport code, Hughes et al. [31]) and the SHIELD-HIT code (Heavy Ion Therapy code, Gudowska et al. [32], Henkner et al. [33]) are well adapted for large scale simulations but are unsuitable for nanometrical modeling. In fact, one common property is that in order to accelerate computing time, small energy transfers, usually below a fixed threshold, are simply skipped in the simulation avoiding the creation of a huge amount of very low energy secondary particles. This is not a problem for large scale calculations as the range of these low energy electrons is of the order of 1 µm as a general assumption and they are considered to be part of the primary particle track. On the nanometrical level this is problematic one would obtain big energy deposit points relatively sparsely distributed in the cell nucleus which is not representative of what happens in reality.

Especially dedicated codes were developed for nanometric scale simulations, we may mention here, PARTRAC (Particle Tracks, see Friedland et al. [8-10]), PITS (Positive Ion Track Simulation, Wilson and Nikjoo [34]), NOREC (National Oak Ridge Electron Transport Code, Semenenko et al. [35]), Geant4-DNA which is an extension to the previously introduced Geant4 code enabling simulations on the DNA scale (Incerti et al. [5]) and others. In these codes an effort is put on simulating almost all dominating interactions that might occur in the cell, however a major approximation is to use water cross sections assuming this it is the major component of biological medium. This approximation was dropped in some codes and DNA cross sections were introduced in calculations [10] offering better and more precise results. For the calculations described in this chapter we used the Geant4-DNA toolkit which is able to simulate tracks of protons, alpha particles, electrons and some heavy ions like Iron and Carbon ions above 1 MeV / amu. Most of the inelastic cross sections are based on the First Born Approximation [36-40] and some semi-empirical models [41, 42]. For sub-keV electrons experimental cross sections [43, 44] were used for vibrational and rotational excitations. We will not go through the details of the cross sections since they can be found in the mentioned references and they are out of the scope of this chapter. In this type of simulations, cross sections take into account all the possible interactions occurring in the medium though the energy threshold cut-off is set to a minimum, meaning that even electrons with energies as low as few eV or less are simulated. Using the numerical simulation we have access to every interaction location and energy loss in the medium which is not the case in experimental procedures where only ionizations can be detected. In fact, in the study of Palajova et al. [45] comparing calculations with experimental results of Borak et al. [46] a small disagreement was observed when all types of interactions were taken into account in the simulations, a better agreement was obtained taking only ionization events. However, for radiobiology studies even non ionizing excitations should be taken into account knowing that such interactions with the DNA components can modify the chemical bindings and lead to a strand break or a base damage. Moreover, the complexity of DNA damage induction can be surprising knowing that electrons below ionizing threshold can still induce resonant DNA breaks as it has been demonstrated by Boudaiffa et al. [47] where electrons of extremely low energies (2 eV- 8 eV) showed to be very effective on DNA. Theoretically these electrons do not have enough energy (above about 8.5 eV) to ionize DNA, however their effect cannot be neglected since they are abundantly created in the medium during irradiation. So the question here remains open since no theoretical models can describe accurately the diffusion of these electrons in water or in biological tissue, depending on the aim of our simulations we might "kill" these electrons below 8 eV and their remaining energy is locally deposited at the end of their track. This of course would change the spatial distribution of the simulated track since we are discarding a certain amount of the "real" interaction points. This "kill" energy threshold can vary from one code to another and from one simulation to another depending on the author assumptions. In what follows our threshold is set to 9 eV, since in the future we consider to study low energy electrons on a side in an independent simulation enhancing the precision of the needed processes.

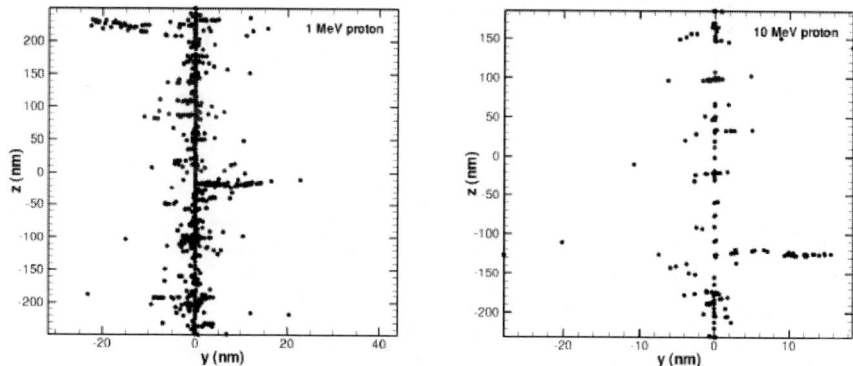

Figure 5. Total interaction points distribution versus track depth for protons of 1 MeV (left) and 10 MeV (right) in water.

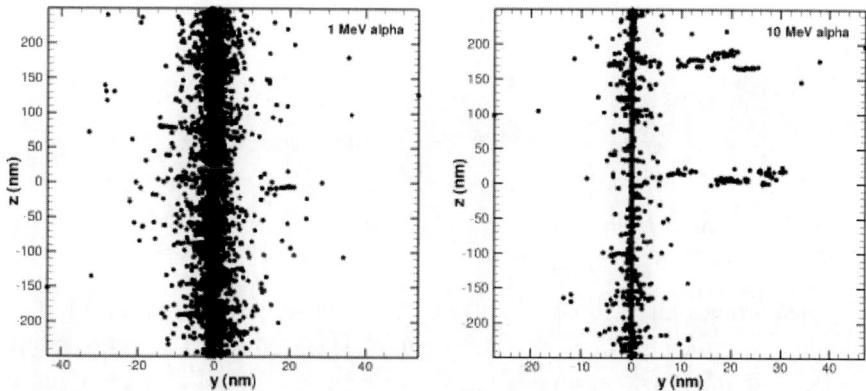

Figure 6. Total interaction points distribution versus track depth for alpha particles of 1 MeV (left) and 10 MeV (right) in water.

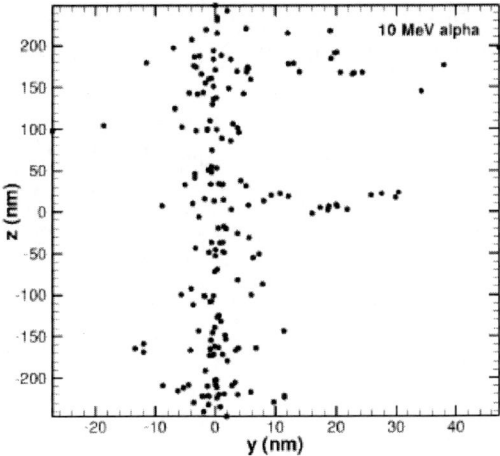

Figure 7. Excitation interactions distribution induced by 10 MeV alpha particles in water.

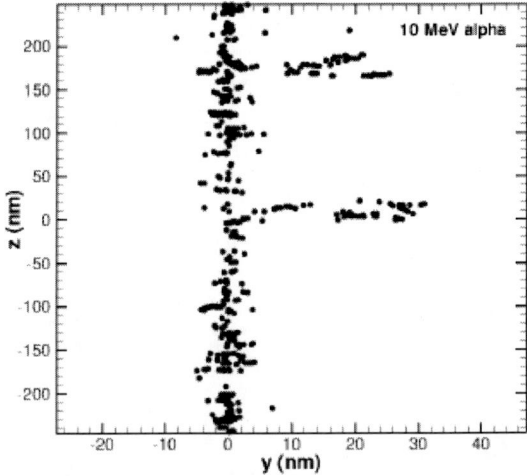

Figure 8. Ionization interactions distribution induced by 10 MeV alpha particles in water.

The particles interactions can also create reactive chemical species in the medium also called free radicals. These radicals can diffuse in the medium and interact with the DNA causing damage to its strands. It is possible to simulate the chemical phase using special cross sections (e.g., Gervais et al. [48]), however in what follows we are not taking into account the chemical processes mainly because our aim is to present quick alternatives for the detailed lengthy calculations by using data mining algorithms. So in some respect we consider that the damage induction and the radiation quality highly depend on the initial distribution of the interaction points in the medium.

Radiation here can be divided into 2 categories; high Linear Energy Transfer (LET) radiation e.g., protons and ions, and low LET radiation e.g., photons and electrons. High LET particles usually induce highly concentrated energy deposit points leading to more concentrated damage in the cell while low LET present more sparsely distributed pattern uniformly distributed in the irradiated volume. Figure 5 shows a track sample of a proton particle crossing a water target. All the interactions locations are shown including ionization and excitation. The comparison shows 2 different energies, 1 MeV which has a higher LET value than the 10 MeV proton. We can easily notice the difference between the interaction concentrations in the 2 cases. Mainly the trajectory of the primary particle is clear along the z axis and for y=0 and the other secondary diffusions around the primary track are induced by secondary electrons that are produced in the medium. Figure 6 shows the same comparison for 1 MeV and 10 MeV alpha particles. In comparison with protons, alpha particles create a denser interaction pattern thus they are expected to be more lethal for the biological cells. This is obviously due to the high interaction probability; actually we expect that the density of the energy deposits increases with increasing ion charge.

Figure 7 shows the excitation process contribution to the interaction points for 10 MeV alpha particles and Figure 8 shows the ionization process contribution. Note that these processes can be induced either by the primary alpha particle or also by the secondary electrons. Note here as a reminder only, ionization points are detected by the experiments and the results can be used to validate somehow part of the simulation.

4. DATA MINING IN RADIOBIOLOGY

After the physical phase simulation, treatment of the obtained results is very author dependent since several methods were published and used depending on the needs of the application. The most detailed approach is to simulate all what is possible from physical interactions, free radicals creation and diffusion, interaction with the DNA molecule taking into account the geometrical structure of the DNA at the atomistic level. This method was mostly explored by Friedland et al. using the PARTRAC code [10] for

2 different DNA models for lymphocyte and fibroblast chromosomes. The results can reveal SSB and DSB counts as well as complex lesions and DNA fragments lengths obtained after the irradiation showing a very good agreements with the experimental data. Other authors published similar studies like Ponomarev et al. [49] while other projects are still in progress exploring some approximate DNA models in an effort to facilitate the computing tasks and improve the computing time. However, this type of calculations is not easily accessible, other methods were developed that can estimate the effectiveness of radiation on DNA and on the molecular level. Generally the whole idea is based on finding the link between the physical track patterns like the examples shown in Figures 5 to 8 and the effect of the particle on living cells. The fastest way that could be used to compare two radiation types is the Hartigan K-means algorithm [50]. By comparing the clustering density of the two radiations one can conclude that the higher the density the more lethal the radiation can be. In a study of Nikjoo et al. [51] using K-means algorithm it was concluded that almost 30 % of the dose was deposited by low energy electrons and the majority of DNA damage lesions are of simple type, also confirming that damage complexity increases with increasing LET. For high LET 70 % of all DSB is of complex type as a general conclusion for protons, alpha particles and carbon ions simulation. For reasons described in previous sections it is very difficult to validate such results by an experiment except from the observation of cell reactions irradiated with different particles. Still no experiment can confirm the clustering density that remains a purely theoretical calculation. The results obtained by the K-means algorithm depend on the starting configuration. For a certain data map, the user has to define the number of clusters that the data will be divided into, and the clusters centers starting positions are first randomly sampled. So running the algorithm in our case would give different results on every run depending on the starting parameters. In the study of Nikjoo et al. [51] the number of clusters was kept constant for the different simulated radiations and the initial particle track was sorted into ascending order along the movement direction of the particle and the N first points were put into the first cluster, the next N points into the second cluster and so on, where N is the initial number of points in a cluster a parameter that is also chosen here by the user. A starting value of 6 points (N=6) was chosen by Nikjoo et al. [51] for their study mentioning that no differences in the results were obtained when choosing a different number.

The study of Nikjoo et al. [51] gives interesting results with clear description on energy deposition clustering but is not adapted for DNA breaks yields estimation. Also another critical point in spite of the initial configuration that was solved by [51], the K-means applicability in this study is affected by the fact that the user has to define the number of clusters at the beginning of the algorithm which is in radiobiology the unknown parameter we are trying to calculate in the first place (among others).

Another idea published by Garty et al. [12] considers a small nanometric dimensions cylinder that is randomly placed on the particle track counting the number of interactions occurring inside of the cylinder. Alternatively, in a simulation one can shoot particles through small cylindrical targets counting the number of the interaction points occurring in the target. In this study, it has been assumed that there is a one-to-one correspondence between the ionizations formed within the target volume and those formed within a DNA segment of equivalent size. Excitations were neglected and the dimensions of the cylinders were chosen to be equivalent to one or two helical turns (~3-8 nm), assuming that two SSB separated by less than such a distance can be considered as a DSB. Distributions of ionizations occurring in such sensitive volumes can be obtained experimentally using a gas tissue equivalent counter or by numerical simulations using a track structure code. Thus the sensitive volume is represented by a cylinder of about ~6 nm of length and ~4 nm of diameter. Assuming also that every single ionization has a fixed probability to be converted into a DNA lesion and an equal chance to fall on one of the two strands, yields of single and double strand breaks can be obtained by the following expressions:

$$G_{SSB} = C \times \frac{\rho.V_{SV}}{W} \times \sum_{n_{ion}} \left\{ f(n_{ion}) \times 2 \left[\left(1 - \frac{p_{SB}}{2}\right)^{n_{ion}} - (1 - p_{SB})^{n_{ion}} \right] \right\} \quad (8)$$

$$G_{DSB} = C \times \frac{\rho.V_{SV}}{W} \times \sum_{n_{ion}} \left\{ f(n_{ion}) \times \left(1 - 2\left(1 - \frac{p_{SB}}{2}\right)^{n_{ion}} + (1 - p_{SB})^{n_{ion}}\right) \right\} \quad (9)$$

where C is a conversion factor, and for C = 9.6 10^{-10} the yield G is obtained in [Gy^{-1} Da^{-1}]. The sensitive volume V_{SV} is in [nm^3], p_{SB} is the probability that an ionization is transformed into a strand break (usually taken between ~9% and ~12%) and W is the mean energy deposited (in eV) by a single event in the sensitive volume.

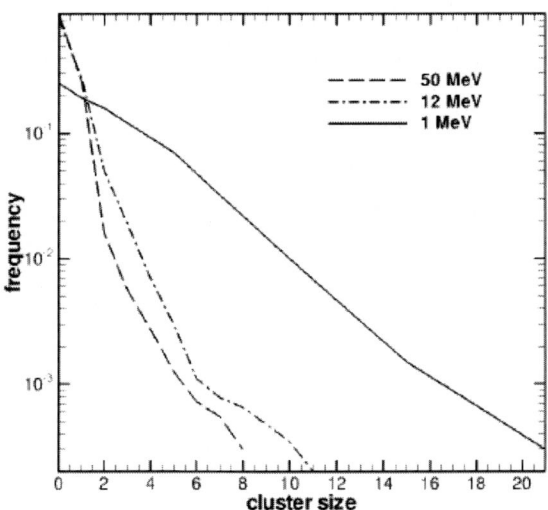

Figure 9. Ionization frequency probability of clusters of different sizes for 1 MeV, 12 MeV and 50 MeV protons crossing nanometric water volume.

$f(n_{ion})$ is the frequency probability of ionization number n_{ion} induced within the sensitive volume for one event. The main advantage here is that the method requires only one input parameter to be fixed by the user, which is the strand break induction probability. For $p_{SB} = 11.7\%$ this approach leads to good agreement with experimental results of gel electrophoresis analysis on plasmid DNA irradiated with electrons and X-rays.

However, since the volume where ionization points are scored keeps the same shape and size during the calculation this method is not suitable for discovering clusters of different shapes. Moreover, in this case, only ionization points are taken into account while it is more accurate to consider also the contribution of the excitation processes, this can be easily concluded through Figure 7.

Numerical simulations of protons with different energies (1 MeV, 12 MeV and 50 MeV) crossing nanometric cylinders were accomplished scoring ionization counts. Figure 9 shows an example of the frequency probability $f(n_{ion})$ for the mentioned proton energies. In fact, when the kinetic energy of the proton increases its linear energy transfer decreases and the resulting deposition points are sparser in the medium. This is seen by the comparison shown in Figure 9 where the highest probability to obtain relatively large clusters (e.g., clusters with more than 10 ionizations) is for 1 MeV protons and this probability decreases when the proton energy increases leading to a mean cluster size of 0.35 points for 50 MeV protons, 0.56 points for 12 MeV protons and 2.8 points for 1 MeV protons.

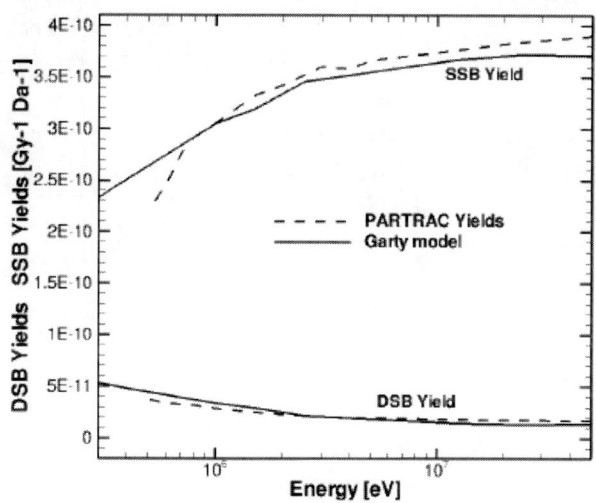

Figure 10. DNA SSB and DSB yields calculated using the method described in Garty et al. [12] and compared to PARTRAC simulations of Friedland et al. [9].

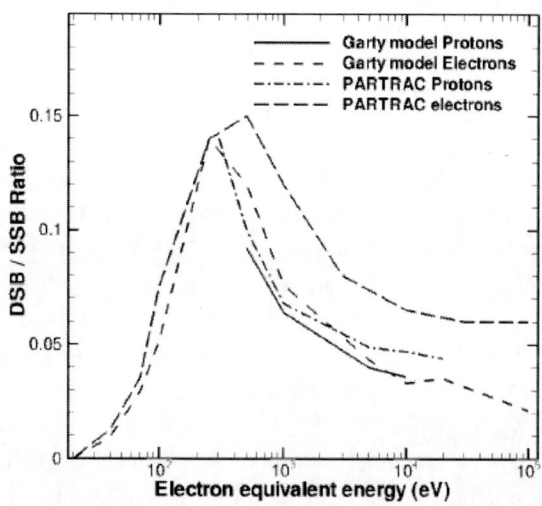

Figure 11. DSB versus SSB yields ratio calculated using Garty method and compared to PARTRAC simulations of Friedland et al. [9]. The results are displayed according to equivalent electron LET values.

In Figure 10 calculations of DNA strand breaks using Garty method are compared to PARTRAC code simulations showing relatively good agreement. The computing time of this method is relatively short, generating tracks in Geant4-DNA takes about 30 minutes for few thousands of proton tracks, and few minutes for the tracks analysis are sufficient. The computing performances depend largely on the particle type and energy since high LET particles are more time consuming to simulate and the hardware capabilities play an important role. The SSB and DSB yields for protons of different energies between 500 keV and 50 MeV are shown; the results are normalized per energy dose unit [Gy] and by DNA mass unit [Da].

Figure 11 shows another comparison of the DSB SSB ratio calculated with the Garty method and the PARTRAC simulations for electrons and protons. The results are reported versus LET equivalent electron energies between 1 eV and 100 keV. The tendency to have electrons ratios higher than protons is due to the fact that the communicated energy to secondary electrons remains small and so their range remains close to the primary particle leading to higher clustering density. This issue was thouroughly discussed for heavy ions in Francis et al. [52].

In spite of the relatively good agreement obtained using Garty method, it can only give an approximation of the yields of SSB and DSB in the medium. If one is interested in other parameters like dimensions of energy deposition clusters of different shapes other clustering methods should be used.

5. USING THE DBSCAN CLUSTERING ALGORITHM

The goal from finding an alternative way to estimate radio-induced DNA damage and/or radiation RBE without going through detailed physical, chemical and geometrical calculations was to provide a more gentle and accessible approach giving quick and acceptable results with reasonable CPU time. To have an approximate idea here a detailed atomistic DNA damage calculation can take several days on a cluster of about 5 CPUs which is cumbersome for immediate applications. Among other methods the K-means is limited and the Garty method works relatively well, but does not give access to spatial dimensions and distributions of clusters of different shapes. Moreover, for clustering methods in radiobiology the energy parameter was not considered, as we have seen so far in the present chapter only the nature of the interaction was taken into account (ionization, excitation or other). The energy deposition amount carries information that might give a hint about the nature of the induced damage or even if there is a damage at all. The minimum amount of energy that we believe can cause a DNA lesion is still an open question under investigations. In fact, the emphasis was always put on ionization transfers where energy deposition exceeded 10.75 eV per interaction point in liquid water. However, recent studies showed that even electrons of low energies (4 eV – 8 eV) can still induce strand breaks to the DNA [47] this is why we considered that the energy parameter should be taken into account, and since we assume that the damage probability may increase with the energy deposition value we introduced a linear probability function that increases accordingly. Practically, below 5 eV we consider a null probability to induce damage, this probability increases and reaches unity at 37 eV. Sequentially, this approach considers a uniform probability for all the points (~16% in our application cases) to fall on a sensitive site on a DNA strand or closely enough to cause a damage, then the damage probability function is used to sample which of the points of the sensitive area are transformed into a damage taking into account the local energy deposition. This first step where damages coordinates and strand location are identified is followed by a second phase where the clustering DBSCAN [14] algorithm is used to identify the potential clusters of damages in the medium. At this stage the algorithm uses 2 parameters that should be fixed in advance; the maximum distance within which neighbor points can form a cluster and the minimum amount of neighbors to form a cluster. Simulations were done with ~3.2 nm as maximum neighboring distance and at least 2 points should be located within this distance to form a cluster. Note that since the DNA molecule has 2 strands, each damage is randomly assigned to one strand with equal probability. In our simulations all possible interactions where taken into account e.g., ionization, excitation, charge transfer, vibrations etc. The obtained clusters of damages were classified into different types as follows:

- SSB are isolated damages with no neighbors;
- DSB are formed by 2 SSBs located on opposite strands;
- Complex SSBs are formed by several SSBs located on one same strand and separated by less than the maximum distance parameter;
- Complex DSBs formed by at least one DSB and one SSB located within the mentioned maximum distance, they can get more complex with increasing concentration of any damage within the mentioned area.

The DBSCAN is well adapted for our kind of applications since it combines different ideas from the previously mentioned approaches for damage estimation. The noise points in our case are nothing but the isolated SSB that are not close enough to each other or to any different damage in order to form a cluster, note here that the noise idea or single point clusters were not really revealed by K-means where every point had to be attributed to a cluster. It is also possible to estimate the average dimensions of clusters by calculating the root mean squared radius and to estimate the concentration of the number of interactions versus the cluster dimensions regardless of the shape of this latter. Another advantage that one can get access to is the spatial distribution of the clusters themselves, actually the clusters positions can give a hint about the sparseness of the lethal/non-lethal damages within the cell.

In spite of the fact that the physical interaction of particles in a biological medium is followed by a complex chemical phase where chemical species are created and diffused within the interaction volume, and also that the geometry and configuration of DNA might play a role in determining the DNA radiosensitivity, we assume that the clustering properties of a certain particle are directly related to its RBE. In fact, DBSCAN was used to estimate yields of DNA DSB and SSB after protons irradiation with energies between 500 keV and 50 MeV [11]. The results were compared to experimental data that were found in the literature. Although the experiments were done for a specific plasmid DNA irradiated with different radiation types (mostly X-rays) the calculation results were in good agreement with the experiments for energies of equivalent proton LET. Moreover, a study by Francis et al. [52] emphasizes on the fact that clustering of energy deposits can be related to radiation relative biological effectiveness (RBE) and a comparison between protons and different heavier ions is presented, showing the different clustering properties of radiations for the same LET. Studies dealing with heavy ions are of interest for hadrontherapy and space radiation applications.

Among different advantages of using the DBSCAN, we might also mention the accelerated computing time, indeed for protons tracks a complete analysis of one or few thousands of tracks (1 µm length each) is of the order of minutes while this time increases with increasing particle charge and LET. This means that for heavy ions like carbon or iron the analysis time is extended and might be relatively lengthy (in hours) although it would never reach the time requirements of atomistic scale simulations.

6. DBSCAN AND GPU TIME ACCELERATION

As fast as the central processing unit (CPU) might be, some applications can still run faster on graphics processing units (GPU) due to the multicore parallel processing technology. Using the Nvidia provided compiler it is possible to process a code in Compute Unified Device Architecture (CUDA). CUDA has many versions compatible with different programming languages, for programs described in this chapter we are using the CUDA C language that is well documented in Sanders et al. [53]. The algorithm version running on CPU is detailed in [11], the basic idea is that clustering procedure can become time consuming for radiations with high interactions density as explained previously. Since at some level during the numerical analysis the program has to calculate all distances separating every point from all the others and checking which of the points fall in the neighboring area. Since this fetch and test method is repeated for every point, the computing time can be quite long and increases exponentially with increasing point number. Although, calculation time in this case is not drastically long for simple cases and remain of the order of few hours, it was however more practical to reduce this time to a minimum in order to make the code ready for more complex cases like heavy ions (e.g., iron, silicon) analysis where the interactions number can exceed by far light ions applications (e.g., protons and alpha particles).

Details about CUDA enabled hardware and architecture are omitted in this paragraph for more information one might check reference [54]. In brief, the user can divide processing tasks between blocks formed by threads. The choice of the number of blocks and threads depends on many parameters like the hardware architecture and how the data is treated through the algorithm itself. Since data here is treated by multicore device, the simplest way to parallelize calculations was to use blocks to treat the different events (an event is a primary particle track with all its secondary particles) in parallel and for each event, energy deposition points are treated in parallel within the block by multiple threads. This way we assume that every thread does the calculation for one point and since the task is multithreaded, multiple points of the same event are treated in parallel while multiple events are also being treated in parallel by different blocks. Running on a GTX 460M Nvidia card (~192 cores) computing time was accelerated by a factor ranging from 22 times to 133 times as maximum performance depending on the studied case. The improvement was taken as the ratio between GPU version calculation time and same case treatment on an i7 quad core CPU. In fact, the clustering itself runs relatively fast, however the delay is mostly caused by the data transfer from the host (random access memory) to the GPU device global memory since before its treatment all data have to be copied onto the device global memory and after calculations are finished the results should be transferred back from the device to the host for display. As an example a sample of 40 events of 1 MeV protons tracks are analyzed in water, the parameters are set to take into account all the interaction points meaning all energy deposition points are considered to induce damages the clustering procedure on CPU takes around 668 seconds while the same procedure took around 15 seconds on GPU. Note that the clustering function itself, meaning if we discard the data reading and writing computing time measures 17 seconds on CPU and 0.126 seconds on GPU which leads to a ratio of 135 times faster. The main difference would be highlighted for high density particles tracks where the ratio between GPU versus CPU computing time is expected to increase further. Calculations were done as a pure investigation matter for future perspectives, however the same programs would run better on a dedicated hardware especially using the Nvidia Tesla cards for better results.

Conclusion

In this chapter radiation damage to DNA was briefly summarized showing few aspects of DNA geometrical and chemical structures. All described simulations were done in liquid water using the Geant4-DNA Monte-Carlo processes of the Geant4 simulation toolkit. The different types of radio-induced DNA damages were presented but could not be completely differentiated in calculations. In fact, for calculations it seems more practical to reason in terms of single or double strand lesions discarding if the lesion is a base damage, strand break or an AP site damage. Ideally, one should be able to differentiate these mentioned damages for a more precise study, however since cross sections are highly dependent on cell type and division cycle among other non-provided parameters. It was not possible to introduce such details at this stage, as a first approximation.

The different methods that are related to or inspired by data mining procedures were presented in an effort to show the link between the energy deposition pattern of an ionizing track and the resulting DNA damage. The chemical reactions were not taken into account directly in this work since the aim was to investigate the link only between the initial particle track signature and its biological effects. Thus classical data mining algorithms are not really exploited in this field related to radiobiology, however other kind of algorithms were developed especially for heavy ions therapeutic purposes [55, 56].

In the DBSCAN approach, although the full chemical diffusion and the DNA geometry modeling were not really taken into account in the simulations, they were accounted for through the different parameters. Mainly we consider that DNA is homogenously occupying 11 % of the nucleus volume and that any energy deposition sufficiently close to DNA can still cause chemical indirect damage through free radicals diffusion. This would mean that we consider a geometrical cross section that an energy deposition could fall in a sensitive area, this cross section is assumed to occupy about 5 % of the nucleus volume and considered as an "aura" around the DNA. This means that at the end 16 % of the irradiated nucleus is considered as sensitive volume. The presented method using DBSCAN is not meant as a replacement for the step by step atomistic simulations but as a fast approximate alternative that needs to be validated for a wider range of applications. Data for low LET photons is relatively available through the literature, however for ions experiments are still difficult to realize especially for ions heavier than alpha, e.g., carbon ions due to the cost of the required installations and the restricted access to such facilities. So the related data is still scarce although strongly needed for the validation of the different developing numerical methods for RBE and DNA damage calculations.

ACKNOWLEDGMENTS

The authors would like to thank the Open University and Professor Nigel J. Mason for their support. ZF is also grateful for the Geant4 low energy electromagnetic group.

REFERENCES

[1] D. J. Brenner, L. R. Hlatky, P. J. Hahnfeldt, et al., The linear-quadratic model and most other common radiobiological models result in similar predictions of time-dose relationships, *Rad. Res.* 150 (1998) 83-91.

[2] A. M. Kellerer, and D. Chmelevsky, Concepts of Microdosimetry I. Quantities, *Rad. Env. Bio.* 12 (1975) 61-69.

[3] A. M. Kellerer, and D. Chmelevsky, Concepts of Microdosimetry II. Probability distributions of the microdosimetric variables, *Rad. Env. Bio.* 12 (1975) 205-216.

[4] T. B. Borak, T. Doke, T. Fuse, et al., Comparisons of L. E. T. distributions for protons with energies between 50 and 200 MeV determined using a spherical tissue-equivalent proportional counter (T. E. P. C.) and a position-sensitive silicon spectrometer (RRMD-III), *Rad. Res.* 162 (2004) 687-692.

[5] S. Incerti, A. Ivanchenko, M. Karamitros, et al., Comparison of GEANT4 very low energy cross section models with experimental data in water, *Med. Phys.* 37 (2010) 4692-4708.

[6] S. Agostinelli, J. Allison, K. Amako, et al., Geant4-a simulation toolkit, *Nucl. Inst. Meth. Phys. Res.* A 506 (2003) 250-303.

[7] J. Allison, et, al., Geant4 developments and applications, *I. E. E. E. Trans. Nuc. Sc.* 53 (2006) 270-278.

[8] W. Friedland, M. Dingfelder, P. Kundrat, et al., Track structures, D. N. A. targets and radiation effects in the biophysical Monte Carlo simulation code P. A. R. T. R. A. C., *Mutat. Res.* 711 (2011) 28-40.

[9] W. Friedland, P. Jacob, P. Bernhardt, et al., Simulation of D. N. A. damage after proton irradiation, *Rad. Res.* 159 (2003) 401-410.

[10] W. Friedland, H. G. Paretzke, F. Ballarini, et al., First steps towards systems radiation biology studies concerned with D. N. A. and chromosome structure within living cells, *Rad. Env. Bio.* 47 (2008) 49-61.

[11] Z. Francis, C. Villagrasa, I. Clairand, Simulation of D. N. A. damage clustering after proton irradiation using an adapted D. B. S. C. A. N. algorithm, *Comp. Meth. Prog. Biomed.* 101 (2011) 265-270.

[12] G. Garty, R. Schulte, S. Shchemelinin, et al., A nanodosimetric model of radiation-induced clustered D. N. A. damage yields, *Phys. Med. Biol.* 55 (2010) 761-781.

[13] Z. Francis, S. Incerti, M. Karamitros, et al., Stopping power and ranges of electrons, protons and alpha particles in liquid water using the Geant4-DNA package, *Nucl. Inst. Meth. Phys. Res.* B 269 (2011) 2307-2311.

[14] J. Sander, M. Ester, H. P. Kriegel, et al., *Density-Based Clustering in Spatial Databases: The Algorithm G. D. B. S. C. A. N. and Its Applications, Data Mining and Knowledge Discovery* 2 (1998) 169-194.

[15] J. D. Watson, F. H. C. Crick, Molecular structure of nucleic acids - a structure of deoxyribose nucleic acid, *Nature* 171 (1953) 737-738.

[16] E. Chargaff, R. Lipshitz, C. Green, et al., The composition of the desoxyribonucleic acid of salmon sperm, *J. Bio. Chem.* 192 (1951) 223-230.
[17] S. Neidle. Principles of nucleic acid structure: New York: Elsevier Inc.; 2008.
[18] J. L. Serre. Diagnostic techniques in genetics: John Wiley and Sons, Ltd.; 2006.
[19] C. Von Sonntag. Free radical induced D. N. A. damage and its repair: New York: Springer; 2006.
[20] A. P. Breen, J. A. Murphy, Reaction of oxyl radicals with D. N. A., *Free Rad. Bio. Med.* 18 (1995) 1033-1077.
[21] S. Ptasinska, B. Bahnev, A. Stypczynska, et al., D. N. A. strand scission induced by a non-thermal atmospheric pressure plasma jet, *Phys. Chem. Chem. Phys.* 12 (2010) 7779-7781.
[22] S. Ptasinska, A. Stypczynska, T. Nixon, et al., X-ray induced damage in D. N. A. monitored by X-ray photoelectron spectroscopy, *J. Chem. Phys.* 129 (2008) 129-134.
[23] A. Stypczynska, S. Ptasinska, B. Bahnev, et al., The influence of amino acids on D. N. A. damage induced by cold plasma radiation. *Chem. Phys. Lett.* 500 (2010) 313-317.
[24] D. Briggs, J. T. Grant. Surface analysis by Auger and X-ray Photoelectron Spectroscopy: Manchester: Surface Spectra I. M. Publications; 2003.
[25] A. W. Czanderna. Methods and Phenomena 1, Methods of surface analysis: Amsterdam: Elsevier Scientific Publishing Company; 1975.
[26] J. C. Vickerman. Surface Analysis, The Principal Techniques: New York: John Wiley and Sons; 1997.
[27] L. De Nardo, P. Colautti, W. Y. Baek, et al., Track nanodosimetry of an alpha particle, *Rad. Prot. Dos.* 99 (2002) 355-358.
[28] L. De Nardo, P. Colautti, V. Conte, et al., Ionization-cluster distributions of alpha-particles in nanometric volumes of propane: measurement and calculation, *Rad. Env. Bio.* 41 (2002) 235-256.
[29] L. De Nardo, P. Colautti, B. Grosswendt, Simulation of the measured ionisation-cluster distributions of alpha-particles in nanometric volumes of propane, *Rad. Prot. Dos.* 122 (2006) 427-431.
[30] B. Grosswendt, S. Pszona, The track structure of alpha-particles from the point of view of ionization-cluster formation in "nanometric" volumes of nitrogen, *Rad. Env. Bio.* 41 (2002) 91-102.

[31] G. Hughes, K. J. Adams, M. B. Chadwick, et al., MCNPX-The L. A. H. E. T. / M. C. N. P. code merger S. A. R. E. 3: Proc. 3rd *Workshop on Simulating Accelerator Radiation Environments (Japan), K. E. K. Proc.* 97-5, June, H/R/D ed H Hirayama (1997) 44-51.

[32] I. Gudowska, N. Sobolevsky, P. Andreo, et al., Ion beam transport in tissue-like media using the Monte Carlo code S. H. I. E. L. D.-H. I. T., *Phys. Med. Biol.* 49 (2004) 1933-1958.

[33] K. Henkner, N. Sobolevsky, O. Jakel, et al., Test of the nuclear interaction model in S H. I. E. L. D-H. I. T. and comparison to energy distributions from G. E. A. N. T. 4, *Phys. Med. Biol.* 54 (2009) 509-517.

[34] W. E. Wilson, H. Nikjoo, A Monte Carlo code for positive ion track simulation, *Rad. Env. Bio.* 38 (1999) 97-104.

[35] V. A. Semenenko, J. E. Turner, T. B. Borak, N. O. R. E. C., a Monte Carlo code for simulating electron tracks in liquid water, *Rad. Env. Bio.* 42 (2003) 213-217.

[36] D. Emfietzoglou, K. Karava, G. Papamichael, et al., Monte Carlo simulation of the energy loss of low-energy electrons in liquid water, *Phys. Med. Biol.* 48 (2003) 2355-2371.

[37] D. Emfietzoglou, H. Nikjoo, Accurate electron inelastic cross sections and stopping powers for liquid water over the 0.1-10 keV range based on an improved dielectric description of the Bethe surface, *Rad. Res.* 167 (2007) 110-120.

[38] M. Dingfelder, D. Hantke, M. Inokuti, et al., Electron inelastic scattering cross sections in liquid water, *Rad. Phys. Chem.* 53 (1998) 1-18.

[39] M. Dingfelder, M. Inokuti, H. G. Paretzke, Inelastic-collision cross-section of liquid water for interactions of energetic protons, *Rad. Phys. Chem.* 59 (2000) 255-275.

[40] M. Dingfelder, L. H. Toburen, H. G. Paretzke. An effective charge scaling model for ionization of partially dressed helium ions with liquid water. The Monte Carlo Method: Versatility Unbounded in a Dynamic Computing World; April 17-21, 2005; Tennessee: American Nuclear Society, LaGrange Park; 2005.

[41] S. G. Kim, W. T. Kim, T. Suzuki, *Phase-field model for binary alloys, Phys. Rev. E Stat. Phys. Plasmas Fluids Relat. Interdiscip.* Topics 60 (1999) 7186-7197.

[42] Y. K. Kim, M. E. Rudd, Binary-encounter-dipole model for electron-impact ionization, *Phys. Rev.* A 50 (1994) 3954-3967.

[43] M. Michaud, L. Sanche, Total cross sections for slow-electron (1-20 eV) scattering in solid H_2O, *Phys. Rev.* A 36 (1987) 4672-4683.

[44] M. Michaud, A. Wen, L. Sanche, Cross sections for low-energy (1-100 eV) electron elastic and inelastic scattering in amorphous ice, *Rad. Res.* 159 (2003) 3-22.
[45] Z. Palajova, F. Spurny, and M. Davıdkova, *Microdosimetry distributions for 40-200 MeV protons Rad. Prot. Dos.* 121 (2006) 376-381.
[46] T. B. Borak, T. Doke, T. Fuse, *et al.*, Comparisons of L. E. T. distributions for protons with energies between 50 and 200 MeV determined using a spherical tissue-equivalent proportional counter (T. E. P. C.) and a position-sensitive silicon spectrometer (RRMD-III), *Rad. Res.* 162 (2004) 687-692.
[47] B. Boudaiffa, P. Cloutier, D. Hunting, et al., Resonnant formation of D. N. A. strand breaks by low-energy (3 to 20 eV) electrons, *Science* 287 (2000) 1658-1660.
[48] B. Gervais, M. Beuve, G. H. Olivera, et al., Numerical simulation of multiple ionization and high L. E. T. effects in liquid water radiolysis, *Rad. Phys. Chem.* 75 (2006) 493-513.
[49] A. L. Ponomarev, R. K. Sachs, Polymer chromosome models and Monte Carlo simulations of radiation breaking D. N. A., *Bioinformatics* 15 (1999) 957-964.
[50] J. A. Hartigan, M. A. Wong, A. K.-Means clustering algorithm, *J. R. Stat. Soc. Ser. C* (Appl. Stat.) 28 (1979) 100-108.
[51] H. Nikjoo, S. Uehara, W. E. Wilson, et al., Track structure in radiation biology: theory and applications, *Int. J. Rad. Bio.* 73 (1998) 355-364.
[52] Z. Francis, S. Incerti, V. Ivanchenko, et al., Monte Carlo simulation of energy-deposit clustering for ions of the same L. E. T. in liquid water, *Phys. Med. Biol.* 57 (2012) 209-224.
[53] J. Sanders, E. Kandrot. C. U. D. A. by example: Addison Wesley; 2011.
[54] D. B. Kirk, W. W. Hwu, editors. Programming Massively Parallel Processors A Hands-on Approach: Morgan Kaufmann; 2009.
[55] M. Kramer, O. Jakel, T. Haberer, et al., Treatment planning for heavy-ion radiotherapy: physical beam model and dose optimization, *Phys. Med. Biol.* 45 (2000) 3299-3317.
[56] M. Kramer, M. Scholz, Treatment planning for heavy-ion radiotherapy: calculation and optimization of biologically effective dose, *Phys. Med. Biol.* 45 (2000) 3319-3330.

In: Data Security, Data Mining ...
Editor: Serge O'Byrne

ISBN: 978-1-62417-582-4
© 2013 Nova Science Publishers, Inc.

Chapter 2

DATA MINING FOR GENOMIC INFORMATION

P. D. Freitas and C. A. Santos[*]

Departamento de Genética e Evolução, Universidade
Federal de São Carlos, São Carlos, SP, Brazil

ABSTRACT

Data mining is an approach used for Knowledge Discovery in Databases (KDD), which is responsible for detecting new and relevant relationships in large amounts of stored data through the development of pattern recognition technologies using statistical and mathematical tools. This method is fast and efficient and is not a particularly recent approach, and it is applicable to statistics, economics, engineering, disease studies in medicine, and other fields. The data are stored electronically, and the search is computerized. Although data mining is still evolving, many areas of study are already using this important resource. In molecular biology, for example, the discovery of molecular markers, such as microsatellites (simple sequence repeats, or SSRs) and single nucleotide polymorphisms (SNPs) using this approach has increased over the last decade in several organisms, such as plants, clams, shrimp and humans. These markers are even more useful when located in expressed regions of the genome, which are known as expressed sequence tags (ESTs).

---

[*] Departamento de Genética e Evolução, Universidade Federal de São Carlos, São Carlos, SP, Caixa Postal 676, CEP 13565-905, Brazil.

Characterizing EST-SSRs and EST-SNPs that may be applicable to genetic studies of economically relevant and threatened species is a useful tool for polymorphism analysis, genetic mapping and quantitative trait loci (QTL) identification.

To identify these markers, owning an EST database (DB) that is capable of data mining is essential. Bioinformatics software eliminates redundancies within each file, and the information generated can be analyzed and regrouped. The ESTs are later submitted to an online DB to search for similarities between the studied sequence (query) and the sequences available online (subject) to elucidate the protein codified by each gene. In shrimp, for example, several highly relevant gene products for homeostasis are highlighted, such as transcription regulatory units and enzyme inhibitors, which links these gene variations, causing different biological responses to stress to EST-SSRs. Data from genomic annotation makes it possible to elucidate a metabolic network, and uniting the fields of genetics and biochemistry to clarify major changes that may be occurring at the cellular level in addition to connecting genotypes to phenotypes. These markers may also be used as biosensors to show particular adaptations to each environment more precisely.

1. Introduction

1.1. The Data Mining Concept

Data mining is a methodology that was developed in the mid-1990s, coming into prominence only in 1994 (Wright, 1998). This method has been used intensively and extensively by financial institutions for (i) credit scoring and fraud detection; (ii) marketers for direct marketing and cross-selling or up-selling; (iii) retailers for market segmentation and store layout, and (iv) manufacturers for quality control and maintenance scheduling. Insights gained from data mining can influence cost, revenue, and operating efficiency while maintaining a high level of care (Koh and Tan, 2005; Yang *et al.*, 2012).

Data mining is defined as the process of discovering patterns in a large amount of data. The process must be automatic or, more often, semiautomatic. The patterns discovered must be meaningful in that they lead to some advantage, usually an economic one, but not in certain other fields, such as molecular biology. The data are invariably present in substantial quantities and are organized in large databases (Wright, 1998; Hall *et al.*, 2011). Data mining concerns solving problems by analyzing the data that is already present to identify valid, novel, potentially useful, and understandable correlations by combing through copious data sets to detect patterns that are too subtle or complex for manual analysis. This method can be defined as the process of finding previously unknown patterns and trends in databases and using that information to build predictive models (Koh and Tan, 2005).

Alternatively, data mining can be defined as the process of data selection and exploration, building models using vast data stores to uncover previously unknown patterns. The related analyses include different disciplines, such as database (DB) management, statistics, and computer science, in addition to artificial intelligence and machine learning (Moore *et al.*, 2010; Hall *et al.*, 2011).

It has been estimated that the amount of data stored in the world's databases doubles every 20 months, and although it would surely be difficult to justify this figure in any quantitative sense, we can all relate to the pace of growth qualitatively (Hall *et al.*, 2011). Data mining techniques can be broadly classified based on what they can do; for instance: (i) description and visualization; (ii) association and clustering; and (iii) classification and estimation, or predictive modeling. The first approach can contribute greatly toward understanding a data set, especially a large one, and detecting hidden patterns in data, mainly complicated ones containing complex and non-linear interactions (Koh and Tan, 2005). With association, the objective is to determine which variables go together, as the most common and important applications in data mining involve predictive modeling (Yang *et al.*, 2012).

Finally, commonly used data mining techniques include traditional statistics, such as multiple discriminant analysis and logistic regression analysis, together with non-traditional methods developed in the areas of artificial intelligence and machine learning (Wright, 1998; Koh and Tan, 2005). In other words, data mining and machine learning methods are much more consistent with the idea of letting the data tell us what the model is, rather than forcing the data to fit a preconceived notion of what a good model is (Moore *et al.*, 2010).

1.2. Mining Biological Data

Within the context of biological science, data mining refers to a bioinformatics approach that combines biological concepts with computer tools and/or statistical methods that are mainly used to discover, select and prioritize targets (Lee *et al.*, 2008). Frequently used mining methodologies to analyze high-throughput data are based on algorithms, which generally include the following steps: normalization - corrects data such that meaningful biological information can be obtained; unsupervised clustering – checks whether there is any pattern or bias in data (samples); and supervised classification – creates a model for the classification of samples (Figure 1) (Yang *et al.*, 2012).

Large amounts of experimental data generated by modern high-throughput technologies are available through various public repositories. Our knowledge of molecular biology, for example, has promoted the growth of information regarding molecular interaction networks and functional biological pathway models. Molecular databases are rapidly expanding and are being organized in lists of DNA, RNA, and protein sequences or functionally related genes (Shindle *et al.*, 2010). As nucleotide sequence databases increase in size, one of the current challenges in bioinformatics is to be able to query them in a sensible way. There are currently many public genomic databases available on the internet. The foremost public databases are GenBank (National Center for Biotechnology Information (NCBI), from the US), EMBL (European Bioinformatics Institute (EBI), from Europe) and DDBJ (DNA Data Bank of Japan, from Japan). The information contained in these databases and others in various formats has a tremendous potential for gaining new insights into the functioning of living systems (Fernandez-Suarez and Birney, 2008; Hall *et al.*, 2011).

Taken together, this approach suggests the importance of data mining, which allows bioinformatics to go beyond simple perusal of genome browsers, such as Ensembl or the UCSC Genome Browser, to address such questions as the biological meaning of the results obtained with a microarray platform or how to identify a short motif upstream of a gene or a large number of molecular markers for population studies (Fernandez-Suarez and Birney, 2008; Brent, 2008).

Another browser that is frequently used to provide biological meaning to DNA sequences is KEGG (Kyoto Encyclopedia of Genes and Genomes – http://www.genome.jp/kegg/). KEGG is the most frequently used DB in bioinformatics for pathway establishment. This database is responsible for integrating genomic and functional information with genomics, chemistry and systematic areas, joining material from data mining to functional data. This integration is observed mainly in pathways, for instance, where the transcriptome project data are referenced in KEGG through Enzyme Commission (EC) numbers, which forecasts the enzymes' behavior in a cell or in an organism on a larger scale (Kanehisa and Goto, 2000; Kanehisa *et al.*, 2008).

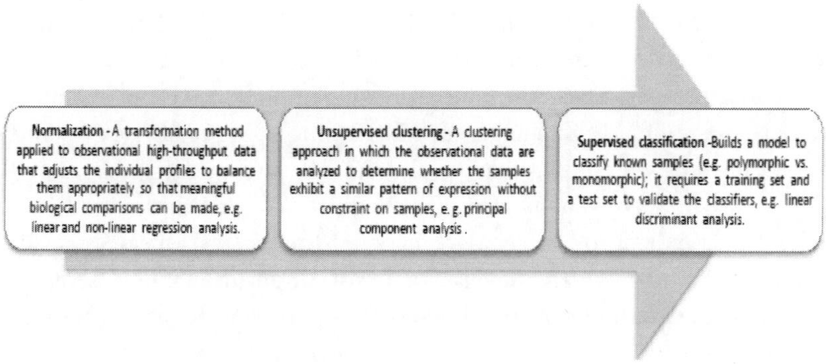

Normalization - A transformation method applied to observational high-throughput data that adjusts the individual profiles to balance them appropriately so that meaningful biological comparisons can be made, e.g. linear and non-linear regression analysis.

Unsupervised clustering - A clustering approach in which the observational data are analyzed to determine whether the samples exhibit a similar pattern of expression without constraint on samples, e.g. principal component analysis.

Supervised classification - Builds a model to classify known samples (e.g. polymorphic vs. monomorphic); it requires a training set and a test set to validate the classifiers, e.g. linear discriminant analysis.

Figure 1. Main steps and algorithms used in data mining analysis based on Yang *et al.*, 2012.

A disadvantage of this tool is that users need to be familiar with the underlying database schema to know where the data are stored. Similarly, performing complex queries may require multiple steps, which can be more laborious with this tool (Koh and Tan, 2005, Yang *et al.*, 2012).

Overall, the focus is on identifying features and developing computational solutions, including algorithms, models, tools, and databases, that can be used for experimental design, data analysis and interpretation, and hypothesis generation. Because data mining is a method for finding trends hidden in large data sets, this approach can be used successfully at all levels of genomic and proteomic analysis.

Thus, we must consider the large amount of data obtained from high-throughput genome and transcriptome projects in the field of molecular biology and find a computational method to extract the wealth of information derived from this data using the most efficient tools available (Blaby-Haas and Crécy-Lagard, 2011). In this way, these data may be applied to gene expression studies and the elucidation of pathways, which requires the development of improved bioinformatics and computational biology tools for efficient and accurate data analyses (Bensmail and Haoudi, 2005).

2. DATA MINING IN GENOMICS

2.1. High-Throughput Data Generation

The beginning of the 21st century has witnessed the generation of spectacular amounts of DNA, RNA and protein sequence data (Brent, 2008;

Lee *et al.*, 2008). This information has been used for microarray experiments, protein interaction network studies, genome meta-analysis and identification of molecular markers. These data are promising approaches for different fields of study (Gotz *et al.*, 2008; Yang *et al.*, 2012), including pharmacy, medicine, nutrition, physics, agriculture, aquaculture, and phylogeny (Kob and Tan, 2005; Fang *et al.*, 2010; Zhang *et al.*, 2010; Hall *et al.*, 2011).

The development of molecular markers for several species has been encouraged by the rapid development of high-throughput sequencing technologies and a number of "low-cost" expressed sequence tag (EST) sequencing projects world-wide, which has generated an increasing quantity of novel, uncharacterized sequence data and created a requirement for fast and reliable functional annotation that would facilitate the biological interpretation of the experiments (Gotz *et al.*, 2008).

To identify potential molecular markers in an efficient way, data mining has been performed in databases from transcriptome projects to identify molecular markers, such as simple sequence repeats (SSRs), or microsatellites, and single nucleotide polymorphisms (SNPs) (Wang *et al.*, 2009; Gorbach *et al.*, 2010; Tsoumani *et al.*, 2011) in a large quantity of data. Both markers are widely used in genetic studies, due to their co-dominant nature and high propensity for detecting polymorphisms in captive or wild populations (Thiel *et al.*, 2003; Liu *et al.*, 2004; Perez *et al.*, 2005; Zeng *et al.*, 2008; Santos *et al.*, 2011).

The markers that are located in genome coding regions, or ESTs, are named EST-SSRs and EST-SNPs and have been highly efficient in (i) polymorphism identification, (ii) metabolism studies when important loci are present in regions responsible for gene control, such as enzymes, (iii) comparative genomics and (iv) quantitative trait loci (QTL) establishment, which allows the development of marker assisted selection (MAS) genetic improvement programs (Christiakov *et al.*, 2006; Bouck and Vision, 2007).

In aquaculture species, such as shrimp, molecular markers have been widely used in MAS programs for promoting the development of superior lineages, mainly for disease resistance and growth. In differential expression studies, SSRs and SNPs were already associated with fitness traits in this group (Mandal and Mukherjee, 2009; Marti *et al.*, 2010).

Genome-wide association studies (GWASs) and testing vast numbers of SNPs independently for correlations to pathogen resistance, for example, could be used with genetic maps to identify subsets of candidate resistance-associated SNPs (Urbach and Moore, 2011). The availability of massive amounts of GWAS data has necessitated the development of new biostatistical methods for quality control, imputation and analysis issues, including multiple testing (Shindle et al., 2010; Blaby-Haas and Crécy-Lagard, 2011).

However, it is now known that most SNPs discovered via GWASs have minor effects on polygenic traits, such as growth, and thus may not be suitable for improving genetic gain. The failure to identify new candidate loci for some traits using GWASs with relatively large sample sizes highlights the limitations of this approach.

We predict that data mining and machine learning methods reveal numerous significant interactions and other complex genotype–phenotype relationships when they are widely applied to GWAS data. The limitations of the linear model and other parametric statistical approaches have motivated the development of data mining and machine learning methods. The advantage of these computational approaches is that they make fewer assumptions concerning the functional form of the model and the effects being modeled (Gotz et al., 2008; Moore et al., 2010).

In human research, the use of microarray analysis made it possible to verify which genes were differentially expressed in cancer patients, depending on the disease stage, which led to improvements in treatment (Lee et al., 2008). However, significant progress also has been made using data mining in vegetal species, such as coffee (*Coffee spp.*), one of the most important agricultural commodities in the world. In the Brazilian Genome Coffee Project, more than 268,000 EST were sequenced, yielding nearly 25,000 potential SNP markers that could be used for genetic studies of this and related species. These studies could contribute to higher productivity rates and more tolerance to pests (Vidal et al., 2010).

2.2. Database Mining and Genomic Annotation

Before the importance of genomic annotation provided a biological meaning for sequence that originated from the genome projects, this process was divided into two main aspects, which are briefly described as (i) gene identification and gene product elucidation and (ii) cellular component and interaction elucidation. Knowledge of the biochemical and physical interactions in the cell allows the establishment of pathways. In the first stage, gene function is determined using several bioinformatics tools, such as those that search for similarities between FASTA sequences, such as the Basic Local Alignment Search Tool (BLAST). This annotation step is the first step in genome construction, and it provides relevant details regarding enzymes and transport proteins. In the second stage, more information is added, such as cellular components that may allow the establishment of pathways or networks (Reed *et al.*, 2006).

Therefore, genomic annotation has identified a significant number of loci with great potential for genetic analysis in several animals and plants (Jiang *et al.*, 2008; Santos *et al.*, 2011; Tsoumani *et al.*, 2011). These markers may be helpful for population genetic studies, monitoring genetic diversity and distance levels of native and captive stocks, identification of important genes and establishment of pathways, thereby yielding a wealth of information for a better understanding of organism physiology (Mukherjee and Mandal, 2009; Marti *et al.*, 2010). These networks highlight the junction of genetic and biochemical data and may clarify the main chemical changes occurring in the cell (Brent, 2008).

To explore the potential of all the information originating from the genome projects and for the determination of biological relevance, functional interpretation of these data is a key step in the analysis, and it cannot be performed without the availability of extensive functional annotation of the datasets (Brent, 2008; Gotz *et al.*, 2008). The most widespread and probably most extensive functional annotation schema for gene and protein sequences is the Gene Ontology (GO) (www.geneontology.org), which has become the standard in almost all public databases. The accurate assignment of functional information to gene products is a complex, laborious and time-consuming task that is often performed manually. Accurate revisions guarantee a high level of annotation correctness (Stein, 2001).

Therefore, genomic high-throughput technologies require automatic functional annotation alternatives to achieve a reasonable degree of biological interpretability. Automatic functional annotation methods rely on sequence, structure, and phylogenetic or co-expression relationships between known and novel sequences.

Function transfer based on sequence similarity is the most extended approach, as it is probably the methodology that best suits the desired high-throughput and high-coverage needs of functional sequence annotation on a genomic scale.

However, function transfer from homologous sequences is comparatively error-prone, and bioinformatics tools in this area should ideally optimize the difficult task of function mining and provide a useful balance between quality and quantity of the transferred knowledge (Gotz *et al.*, 2008; Gianoulis *et al.*, 2009).

Thus, there is an increasing need for bioinformatics resources that are able to cope with large amounts of sequence data, produce valuable annotation results and make the data easily accessible to laboratories where functional genomics projects are being undertaken (Shindle *et al.*, 2010; Urbach and Moore, 2010).

Several DBs provide biological information about proteins in a reasonable manner and, more specifically, concerning enzymes, such as the ExPASy Proteomics Server (expasy.org), KEGG and BRENDA (www.brenda-enzymes.info), which provide more details about protein activities and interactions with other molecules. Certain data from these DBs are more reliable than others, and the DBs based on enzymatic activity tend to be more reliable compared to those based on sequence similarity alone (Reed *et al.*, 2006). Data regarding proteins, such as cellular components, molecular function and biological processes, can be obtained from other sources, such as SwissProt (http://expasy.org/sprot/) and Gene Ontology (Yamanishi *et al.*, 2009).

2.3. Enzymatic Pathways and their Applications

Among the relevant data obtained from the genomic annotations performed in online DBs, as observed previously, are the EC numbers, which can be defined as enzyme identification codes. These numbers have an essential role in computational representations of enzymatic reactions in a network, showing a basically hierarchical classification of the reactions involved (Yamanishi *et al.*, 2009). One of the major databases that have been used to determine EC numbers is KEGG, which is characterized by its ability to join genomic and functional information. The genomic data are stored in the GENES database, which contains a current list of all partial and complete genomes.

However, information about gene function is available in the PATHWAY database, which contains graphical representations of many biological processes, e.g., metabolism. Both assemblies can be represented by enzymatic pathways with the EC numbers connecting them, and bioinformatics tools are essential for this process (Kanehisa and Goto, 2000; Kanehisa *et al.*, 2008).

Therefore, data originating from genomic annotation makes it possible to elucidate a metabolic network by joining genetic and biochemical fields to clarify changes that are occurring at the cellular level in addition to connecting genotypes to phenotypes. These markers may also be used as biosensors, to more easily highlight the disorders experienced by a population and consequent adaptations and phenotypic feedback observed in certain restricted environments. Sets of pathways together constitute the metabolic networks, and allow us an even wider perspective of proteins and their interactions (Gianoulis *et al.*, 2009; Tu *et al.*, 2010; Santos *et al.*, in press). Considerable progress will be made in genomics with experimental association studies, defined as experiments aimed at detecting functional links between proteins, which can be inferred from the co-expression of genes or the detection of physical interactions between proteins.

The assumption is that proteins that are co-expressed or interact with each other belong to the same pathway or have similar functions in the cell. Meta-analysis of gene expression includes two approaches. The first is co-expression meta-analysis, which is the analysis of co-expressed genes across species. Confidence that two genes are involved in the same pathway or process is gained by observing that gene A and gene B are co-expressed in species 1, and the homologs of genes A and B are co-expressed in species 2. Further confirmation is gained when the members of a gene family are induced under similar conditions in several species (Gianoulis *et al.*, 2009); Blaby-Hass and Crécy-Lagard, 2011).

Particularly, the combination or integration of text mining with high-throughput data analysis, such as with genomic and proteomic data, has been increasingly used with success in other fields, such as searching for disease markers and drug targets. For example, the data generated from data mining have identified their target through therapeutic and diagnostic tests and validated their insertion in pathways. Once the role and location of the target in the cell is known, drugs are developed and tested to produce new medicines for treatment (Koh and Tan, 2005).

Indeed, data mining has already been widely applied to identify targets for therapeutic invention and early diagnosis. Due to its potential importance, this approach will inevitably become the first phase of future drug discovery pipelines by helping to select proper targets and better understand the targets' cellular mechanisms (Yang *et al.*, 2012).

The continued growth of gene-gene and protein-protein interaction data have enabled scientists to analyze and visualize a variety of datasets in the context of biological networks or pathways, mainly with a manually curated knowledge base, such as KEGG, and experimental interactome tools that mine high-throughput expression data based on precise pathway knowledge bases. In addition, this approach allows the mapping of expression profiles of genes or proteins simultaneously onto major regulatory, metabolic and cellular pathways (Kanehisa and Goto, 2000; Kanehisa *et al.*, 2008; Gianoulis *et al.*, 2009; Yang *et al.*, 2012). Data mining in genomics and proteomics studies reveals new regulatory pathways and mechanisms in different health and disease conditions. According to Lee *et al.* (2008), many recent pathway modeling studies for transcriptional regulation and gene functional networks have been performed based on genomic expression data. These approaches can be largely divided into three categories—qualitative, quantitative, and integrative pathway modeling—based on the different types of genomic data that are used, as described below:

I   Qualitative Pathway Modeling - Pathway modeling that has been carried out using functional and annotation information from several genomic databases. For example, computationally predicting genome-wide transcription units based on pathway-genome databases. No gene expression data are considered.

II Quantitative Pathway Modeling - Gene regulation networks have also been explored based on quantitative genomic expression data. For example, Bayesian network modeling was used for capturing regulatory interactions between genes based on genome-wide expression measurements. These quantitative pathway models have been found to characterize both relationships and magnitude of relevant gene expression patterns effectively and have been used extensively in recent pathway modeling in various microarray studies.

III Integrative Pathway Modeling - Integration of qualitative and quantitative gene network information has been attempted in recent pathway modeling studies. This method combines the known motif structural information and gene expression patterns based on an integrated regression analysis. For example, regression on transcription motifs is proposed for discovering sequences upstream of candidate genes that undergo expression changes under various biological conditions.

This large and rapidly increasing compendium of data demands data mining approaches and ensures that genomic data mining will continue to be a necessary and highly productive field for the foreseeable future. Mining this data has been a productive avenue for generating new hypotheses, as well as validating experimental results (Lee *et al.*, 2008; Shindle *et al.*, 2010).

CONCLUSION

Benefits and Challenges

Data mining can be limited by the accessibility of data because the raw inputs for data mining often exist in different settings and systems, such as administration, clinic, laboratory, and genomic projects or databases. Hence, the data have to be collected and integrated before data mining can be performed. Other data problems may arise, including missing, corrupted, inconsistent, or non-standardized data, such as pieces of information recorded in different formats or in different data sources. The quality of data mining results and applications depends on the quality of the data. A sufficiently exhaustive mining of data will certainly yield certain patterns that are a product of random fluctuations. This phenomenon is especially true for large data sets with many variables (Koh and Tan, 2005; Moore et al., 2010).

Unfortunately, data mining projects can fail for a variety of reasons, such as lack of management support, unrealistic user expectations, poor project management and inadequate data mining expertise. Data mining requires intensive planning and technological preparation work (Koh and Tan, 2005). In addition, physicians, biologists and all parties involved in the data mining effort have to cooperate, as the successful application of data mining requires a wide knowledge of the domain area, as well as methodology and tools. Without a sufficient knowledge of data mining, the user may not be aware of or be able to avoid the pitfalls of data mining (Lee et al., 2008). Other challenges to be overcome in data mining are listed in Table 1.

Keeping these challenges in mind, future work should be directed towards the development of integrated databases in uniform formats and using biologist-friendly software or tools for routine use to accelerate target discovery (Shindle et al., 2010). Workflows and pipeline systems should be deployed to facilitate these searches. We have every reason to believe that data mining will play an increasingly significant part in future biomarker and drug discovery campaigns. Data mining approaches will become the first phase of future drug discovery pipelines by helping to select proper targets and better understand the cellular mechanisms or phenotypes across many animal groups (Yang et al., 2012).

Currently, different platforms contain notably consistent information for many gene expression patterns such that we can successfully perform our investigations across those different genomic data sets.

Table 1. Other frequent issues found in Data Mining approach based on Lee *et al.*, 2008

Challenge 1: Multiple comparisons issue – Several patterns and/or algorithms may result in a high false-negative error rate with failure to identify many important real biological targets.
Challenge 2: High dimensional biological data – Many genomic studies contain high dimensional biological data. In genomic data analysis, many gene targets are investigated simultaneously, yielding dramatically sparse data points in the corresponding high-dimensional data space. It is well-known that mathematical and computational approaches often fail to capture such high dimensional phenomena accurately. Data mining must convert high dimensional data problems into lower dimensional ones, or important variation and information in the biological data may be obscured. The analysis should be limited to a precise number of variables.
Challenge 3: Computational limitation – As seen above, no matter how powerful a computer system becomes, it is often limited in solving many genomic data mining problems by exhaustive combinatorial search and comparisons.
Challenge 4: Noisy high-throughput biological data – High-throughput biotechnical data and large biological databases are inevitably noisy because biological information and signals of interest are often obscured by many other random or confounding factors. In particular, the distributional characteristics of each data set need to be analyzed using statistical and quality control techniques on initial data sets such that relevant statistical approaches may be applied appropriately. Large databases must also be compounds of smaller and simpler bases for research.
Challenge 5: Integration of multiple, heterogeneous biological data for translational – The last challenge is the integration of genomic data with heterogeneous biological data and associated metadata, such as gene function, biological phenotypes and pathways. For example, as could be observed, multiple heterogeneous data sets, including gene expression data and biological responses, need to be combined to discover genomic biomarkers and gene networks. A number of these data sets exist in notably different formats and may require optimization, depending on their biological characteristics and data distributions. Effective combination and utilization of the information from such heterogeneous genomic and other data resources remains a significant challenge.

One way to facilitate close collaboration between biologists, biostatisticians and bioinformaticians is to make user-friendly software packages available that can be used jointly by researchers with expertise in experimental biology and researchers with expertise in statistics and computer science (Moore, 2007). This approach will require software that is intuitive enough for a biologist and powerful enough for an analyst. To be intuitive to a biologist, the software needs to be easy to use and needs to provide output that is visual and easy to navigate. To be powerful, the software needs to provide the functionality that would allow a biostatistician and a bioinformatician the flexibility to explore the more theoretical aspects of the algorithm (Lee *et al.*, 2008; Moore *et al.*, 2010).

Post-genomic science is producing vast data torrents. It is common knowledge that data do not equal knowledge; therefore, the extraction of the most meaningful parts of these data is key to the generation of useful new knowledge (Brent, 2008).

More sophisticated data mining strategies are needed for mining such high-dimensional data and generating useful relationships, rules, and predictions (Lee *et al.*, 2008; Bensmail and Haoudi, 2005).

Acknowledgments

The authors wish to thank Universidade Federal de São Carlos (UFSCar), Conselho Nacional de Desenvolvimento Científico e Tecnológico (CNPq), Coordenação de Aperfeiçoamento de Pessoal de Nível Superior (Capes) and Fundação de Amparo à Pesquisa do Estado de São Paulo (FAPESP) for their support.

References

Bensmail, H. and Haoudi, A. (2005). Data mining in genomics and proteomics. *Journal of biomedicine and biotechnology*, 2, 63-64.

Blaby-Haas, C. E. and Crécy-Lagard, V. (2011). Mining high-throughput experimental data to link gene and function. *Trends in biotechnology*, 29, 174-82.

Bouck, A. and Vision, T. (2007). The molecular ecologist' s guide to expressed sequence tags. *Molecular Ecology*, 907-924.

Brent, M. R. (2008). Steady progress and recent breakthroughs in the accuracy of automated genome annotation. *Nature reviews. Genetics*, 9, 62-73.
Chistiakov, D. A., Hellemans, B. and Volckaert, F. A. M. (2006). Microsatellites and their genomic distribution, evolution, function and applications: A review with special reference to fish genetics. *Aquaculture*, 255, 1 - 29.
Fernández-Suárez, X. M. and Birney, E. (2008). Advanced genomic data mining. *PLoS computational biology*, 4(9), e1000121.
Gorbach, D. M., Hu, Z.-L., Du, Z.-Q., and Rothschild, M. F. (2010). Mining ESTs to determine the usefulness of SNPs across shrimp species. *Animal biotechnology*, 21(2), 100-3.
Götz, S., García-Gómez, J. M., Terol, J., Williams, T. D., Nagaraj, S. H., Nueda, M. J., Robles, M., et al. (2008). High-throughput functional annotation and data mining with the Blast2GO suite. *Nucleic acids research*, 36(10), 3420-35.
Hall, M. A., Witten, I. H., Frank, E. (2011). *Data Mining*. Pratical Machine Learning Tools and Techniques. Third Edition. Burlinton. US. Elsevier.
Jiang, H., Cai, Y.-M., Chen, L.-Q., Zhang, X.-W., Hu, S.-N., and Wang, Q. (2008). Functional annotation and analysis of expressed sequence tags from the hepatopancreas of mitten crab *(Eriocheir sinensis)*. *Marine biotechnology* (New York, N.Y.), 11(3), 317-26.
Kanehisa, M. and Goto, S. (2000). KEGG: kyoto encyclopedia of genes and genomes. *Nucleic acids research*, 28(1), 27-30.
Kanehisa, Minoru, Araki, M., Goto, S., Hattori, M., Hirakawa, M., Itoh, M., Katayama, T., et al. (2008). KEGG for linking genomes to life and the environment. *Nucleic acids research*, 36 (Database issue), D480-4.
Koh, H. C. and Tan, G. (2005). Data mining applications in healthcare. *Journal of healthcare information management : JHIM*, 19(2), 64-72.
Lee, J. K., Williams, P. D. and Cheon, S. (2008). Data mining in genomics. *Clinics in laboratory medicine*, 28(1), 145-66.
Liu, Z. J. and Cordes, J. F. (2004). DNA marker technologies and their applications in aquaculture genetics. *Aquaculture*, 238(1-4), 1-37.
Marti, S. M., Onteru, S. K., Du, Z. Q., and Rothschild, M. F. (2010). Short communication . SNP analyses of the 5HT1R and STAT genes in Pacific white shrimp , *Litopenaeus vannamei*. *Spanish Journal of Agricultural Research,* 8(1), 53-55.
Moore, J. H. (2007) Bioinformatics. *Cell Physiology*, 213, 365–369.

Moore, J. H., Asselbergs, F. W. and Williams, S. M. (2010). Bioinformatics challenges for genome-wide association studies. *Bioinformatics* (Oxford, England), 26(4), 445-55.

Mukherjee, K., M. N. (2009). A Microsatellite DNA Marker Developed for Identifying Disease-resistant Population of Giant Black Tiger Shrimp, *Penaeus monodon*. *Journal Of The World Aquaculture Society*, 40(2), 274-280.

Reed, J. L., Famili, I., Thiele, I., and Palsson, B. O. (2006). Towards multidimensional genome annotation. Nature reviews. *Genetics*, 7(2), 130-41.

Santos, C. A, Rossini, B. C., Marques, C. G., Galetti, P. M., and Freitas, P. D. (2011). Characterization and genomic annotation of polymorphic EST-SSR loci in *Litopenaeus vannamei* shrimp. *Aquaculture Research*, 1-4.

Shinde, K., Phatak, M., Johannes, F. M., Chen, J., Li, Q., Vineet, J. K., Hu, Z., et al. (2010). Genomics Portals: integrative web-platform for mining genomics data. *BMC genomics*, 11, 27.

Stein, L. (2001). reviews genome annotation: from sequence to biology. *Genetics*, 2 (July).

Thiel, T., Michalek, W., Varshney, R. K., Graner, A. (2003). Exploring EST databases for the development and characterization of gene-derived SSR-markers in barley (*Hordeum vulgare*). *Theoretical Applied Genetics*. 106, 411-422.

Tsoumani, K. T., Augustinos, A. A., Kakani, E. G., Drosopoulou, E., Mavragani-Tsipidou, P., and Mathiopoulos, K. D. (2011). Isolation, annotation and applications of expressed sequence tags from the olive fly, *Bactrocera oleae*. Molecular genetics and genomics: *MGG*, 285(1), 33-45.

Tu, H. T., Silvestre, F., Phuong, N. T., and Kestemont, P. (2010). Effects of pesticides and antibiotics on penaeid shrimp with special emphases on behavioral and biomarker responses. *Environmental toxicology and chemistry / SETAC*, 29(4), 929-38.

Urbach, D. and Moore, J. H. (2011). The spatial dimension in biological data mining. *BioData mining*, 4(1), 6. BioMed Central Ltd.

Valles-Jimenez, R., Cruz, P., Perez-Enriquez, R. (2005). Population Genetic Structure of Pacific White Shrimp *(Litopenaeus vannamei)* from Mexico to Panama: Microsatellite DNA Variation. *Marine biotechnology* (New York, N.Y.), 6, 475-484.

Vidal, R. O., Mondego, J. M. C., Pot, D., Ambrósio, A. B., Andrade, A. C., Pereira, L. F. P., Colombo, C. A., et al. (2010). A high-throughput data mining of single nucleotide polymorphisms in *Coffea* species expressed sequence tags suggests differential homeologous gene expression in the allotetraploid *Coffea arabica*. *Plant physiology*, 154(3), 1053-66.

Wang, X., Guo, X., Zhang, Y., Meng, X., Qiu, X., Liu, S., and Zhang, S. L. T. (2009). Development of polymorphic EST-derived SSR markers for the shrimp, *Fenneropenaeus chinensis*. *Conservation Genetics*, 1455-1457.

Wright, P. (1998). Knowledge Discovery In Databases: Tools and Techniques.

Yamanishi, Y., Hattori, M., Kotera, M., Goto, S., and Kanehisa, M. (2009). E-zyme: predicting potential EC numbers from the chemical transformation pattern of substrate-product pairs. *Bioinformatics* (Oxford, England), 25(12), i179-86.

Yang, Y., Adelstein, S. J. and Kassis, A. I. (2012). Target discovery from data mining approaches. *Drug discovery today*, 17 Suppl. (February), S16-23. Elsevier Ltd.

Zeng, D., Chen, X., Li, Y., Peng, M., Ma, N., Jiang, W., Yang, C., et al. (2008). Analysis of HSP 70 in *Litopenaeus vannamei* and detection of SNPs. *Journal of Crustacean Biology*, 28(4), 727-730.

Zhang, R., Zhu, A., Wang, X., Yu, J., Zhang, H., Gao, J., Cheng, Y., et al. (2010). Development of *Juglans Regia* SSR Markers by Data Mining of the EST Database. *Plant Molecular Biology Reporter*, 28(4), 646-653.

In: Data Security, Data Mining ... ISBN: 978-1-62417-582-4
Editor: Serge O'Byrne © 2013 Nova Science Publishers, Inc.

Chapter 3

DATA MANAGEMENT IN THE SEMANTIC WEB

Lubos Matejicek
Institute for Environmental Studies, Charles University in Prague,
Faculty of Natural Science, Prague, Czech Republic

ABSTRACT

Data management encompasses a number of professions that are generally focused on the development, execution and supervision of plans, policies, programs and practices that control, protect, deliver and enhance the value of data and information assets. In the framework of this delineation, Geographic Information Systems (GISs) together with cloud computing represent an emerging computing paradigm, which offers delivering a variety of computing services in a way that has not been experienced previously. In order to develop advanced data management, standard systems must be adapted to more powerful and efficient computing tools. A few examples are used to demonstrate a new way of data management using GIS and cloud computing tools. The examples are dealing with processing of satellite images and aerial photographs that are complemented by spatial objects linked tothe geodatabase. The attached examples also demonstrate the use of cloud-computing tools for data management and semantic web services. It can support decision-making processes in the areas of interest, and indicate potential solutions for other research fields of study. Data management using cloud computing and GIS represents a new application domain that outlines new means in research, and new trends in education. It promises to provide opportunities for delivering a variety of advanced computing services focused on data management. Besides GIS data management, the chapter also describes basic spatial data formats, spatial web basedservices, and new developments based on the geodatabase and its data models. Sharing spatial and temporal data via Internet includes description of the web based services for spatial data management based on the Open Geospatial Consortium (OGC) standards implemented, as examples, inthe Map Server and in the ArcGIS server.

Keywords: Database management; GIS; cloud computing; geodatabase; spatial web services

1. INTRODUCTION

Our interaction with objects in the world is diverse, and can be described in many ways. Most often, spatial objects are presented in the form of maps and symbols. Looking at a map gives us the knowledge of where objects are, and how they are linked to their environment. Most often, Geographic Information Systems (GIS) are used to provide a spatial framework to support decisions for the intelligent use of earth'sresources and to manage the man-made environment. A GIS can manage information through an interactive session with maps on personal computers that reveal information that is not apparent on printed maps.In addition to querying all known attributes of features, spatial relations can be explored by querying topological attributes [1, 2]. For example, users can create a list of objects connected from one point on a network to another, and perform analysis to explore phenomena such as water flow, travel time, or dispersion of pollutants. A spatial data model in GIS is represented by an abstraction of the real world that employs a set of data objects that support map display, query, editing and analysis. Data formats used for representations include features, networks, locations, surfaces and images. Features represent discrete objectssuch as points, lines and polygons. A network is a more complex structure with a set of features that participate in a linear system such as a utility network, stream network, or road network. Locations are represented by addresses, space coordinates, postal codes, place names or route locations. The earth's surface can be based on a few data formats such as a triangulated irregular network (TIN), as elevation values on cells in a raster, or as contour lines. Images derived from aerial photographs or satellite scenes often provide an informative background display below feature layers [3].

The use of spatial data models in GIS varies widely, according to the type of application. However, applications do have in common the need for a system that provides the following minimum of functions focused on data input and verification, data storage and management, data output and presentation, data transformation, and interaction with end users. Computer programs dealing with spatial objects are able to handle most of these tasks by their own build-in functions. In case of GIS, the kernel is based on a database management system (DBMS) handling the storage and management of the data, as well as interaction with users. In order touse efficiently such a system, the spatial objects of interest have to be modeled, which includes simplifications, selection of typical characteristics, and finding of appropriate structures to store all the data. The traditional database is dealing with a large collection of interrelated data stored within a computer environment. The data have to be persistent, which means that it survives unexpected software or hardware problems. Frequent applications of databases include data management of banking, travel reservations, or residents. In order to provide basic data management, DBMS is used to manage the database structure and control access to data stored in a database such as defining, constructing, manipulating, querying and updating. A DBMS operates as a mediator between application programming tools and the devises where the data resides. It contains a few parts that are focused on processing queries, control access and data management. The datamanagement represents the lower part that allows one to access both the data itself and the metadata necessary to describe the structure of the database, Figure 1. It represents the fundamental concept of data independence that allows users to interact with data independently of the actual physical storage. The DBMS is in charge of translating the data requirements from the application programming tools into efficient operations on physical data structures. Thus, a few levels of abstraction in the framework of data management are achievable in comparison to file processing, in which the structure of a file, together with data access functions, are directly implemented in an access program. The physical level is devoted to the storage structures. The logical level deals with the data representation based on user requirements. The external level is linked to applications such as local program tools and web based applications. Data management within a DBMS is mostly provided through expressing queries, creating data tables, inserting or updating data, definition of access rules, and so on. It is implemented in the framework of the data manipulation languages. One of the most useful languages is represented by structured query language (SQL) that is uniformly used in all relational systems based on fairly simple structures such as the table or relation. The SQL is accessible to non-expert users, who do not need to be aware of how the tasks are processed. This language is declarative and the set of data manipulations is precisely defined by relational calculus and relational algebra. The counterpart to SQL simplicity is less sufficiency in time consuming spatio-temporal analyses in comparison to programming languages such as C that can provide numerical calculation in a more efficient way. In addition to standard software application extensions, the DBMS offers efficient way to support geospatial data on condition that database can store both spatial and alphanumeric data. In order to support spatial applications, the DBMS requires a few extensions such as an extension of the logical data representation to geometric data, an extension of the SQL by new operations applicable to geometric objects, efficient management of the spatial data on the physical level, and efficient data access for application programs and web based applications [4].

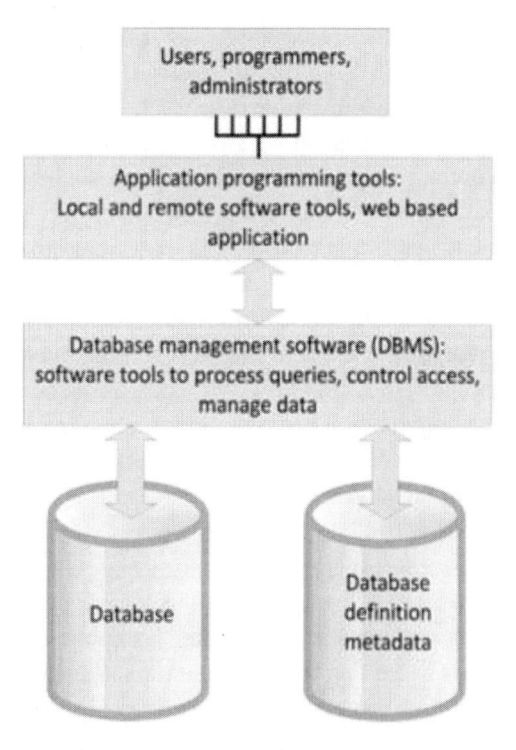

Figure 1. The environment of a DBMS in the framework of data management.

Geospatial data manipulations in GIS are based on spatial objects organized into themes that contain the geospatial information corresponding to a particular topic such as cities, roads, rivers, countries and so on. Spatial objects linked to entities of the real world have two components that are represented by alphanumeric attributes, a set of descriptive attributes such as names or addresses, and by spatial components that embody both geometry and topology. In order to provide database management, the extensions of the DBMS are mainly focused on operations of projection, extraction, overlay, proximity, spatial statistics, data conversion, and other sets of functions integrated in an advanced spatial analyses, 3D analyst tools, and network analyst tools.

2. GEODATABASE

Objects and their interactions in the world are diverse, and can be modeled in many ways. The very first computerized systems were based on Computer-Aided Design (CAD). The CAD data model mainly manages data through the binary file formatswith representations for points, lines, and areas, likewise scan information in images and annotation labels.

The more advanced data model was introduced by Environmental Systems Research Institute, Inc. (ESRI) in the framework of its first commercial GIS software ArcInfo in 1981. The software ArcInfo implemented a second generation geographic data model, the coverage data model. The key facets represent combined storage of spatial data and attributes, anda possibility to complement data with topological relationships between vector features.

A new object-oriented data model, the geodatabase data model was implemented in ArcInfo 8. The geodatabase serves as the common data storage and management framework for ESRI's ArcGIS. It can be leveraged in various GIS computing environments such as a desktop GIS, a server GIS or mobile applications via a local user interface or web based systems, Figure 2. The geodatabase can store a rich collection of spatial data with application of sophisticated rules and relationships in a centralized location. The storage of features and rules is created in the framework of advanced geospatial relational models that maintain integrity of spatial data with a consistent, accurate database. The primary goals of the models is to provide a series commonly used GIS datasets by applying best practices for GIS data modeling and collection. Thus, users have a series of recipes or templates for implementing geodatabase for specific solutions.

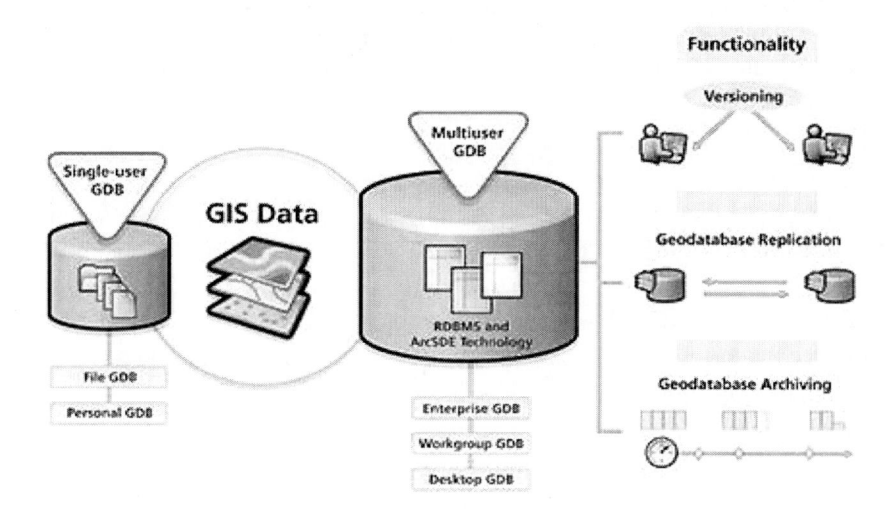

Figure 2. The geodatabase as the common data storage and management framework (http://www.esri.com/software/arcgis/geodatabase, July 25th 2012).

Data models are built to be open for data sharing and interchange of data between GIS and other systems. They use commonly adopted spatial representations such as points, lines and polygons, and specify the integrity rules for key data layers and feature classes. The data models managed by ArcGIS can be widely adopted regardless of the system architectures and the used DBMS.

Data models can be downloaded via the web site supported by ESRI (http://support.esri.com/en/downloads/datamodel, July 25th 2012) together with case studies and design templates [5, 6].

3. DATA MODELS: EXAMPLES

The first example of a data model is focused on surface water modeling. The model was complemented by the ArcGIS project, Figure 3. The attached catalog window shows the structure of the data model in more detail as a list of thematic layers and relationalclasses.

The second example is dealing with geological mapping. Again, the data model was complemented by the ArcGIS project, Figure 4. The attached catalog window shows the structure of a data model in more detail as a list of thematic layers and relational classes that define relationship class properties for the relation between the attribute tables and external data tables.

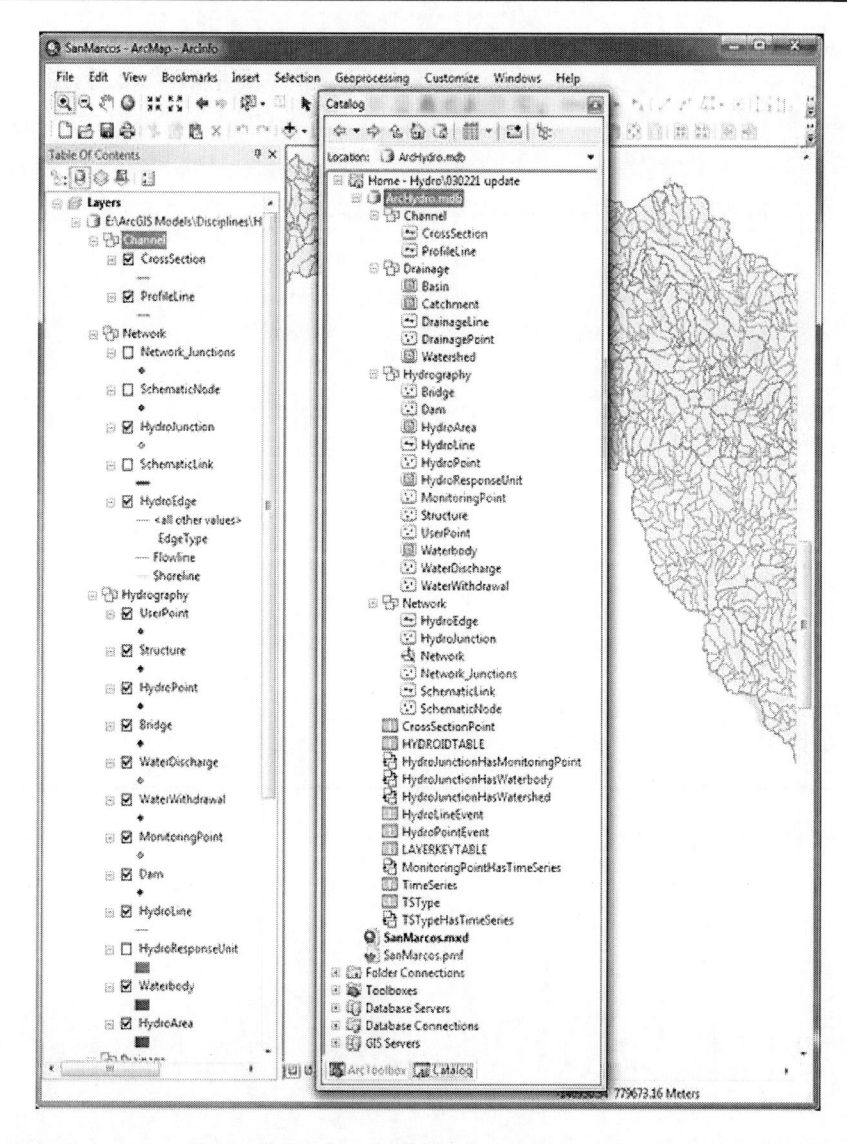

Figure 3. An example of a hydro data model in the catalog window complemented by the ArcGIS project in the background (http://support.esri.com/en/downloads/data model/detail/15, July 25th 2012).

The geodatabase design is provided in order to support a huge set of functions and methods implemented in the ArcGIS and its extensions such as the 3D Analyst, the Spatial Analyst, the Network Analyst, the Geostatistical Analyst and so on [7, 8, 9]. The results of spatial analyses stored in a geodatabase are directly accessible by other application programs without even going through the ArcGIS. Thus the data, for example for hydrologic modeling can be accessed using at least four different interfaces: ArcGIS, Microsoft Access, Microsoft Excel, and by programming Visual Basic [10].

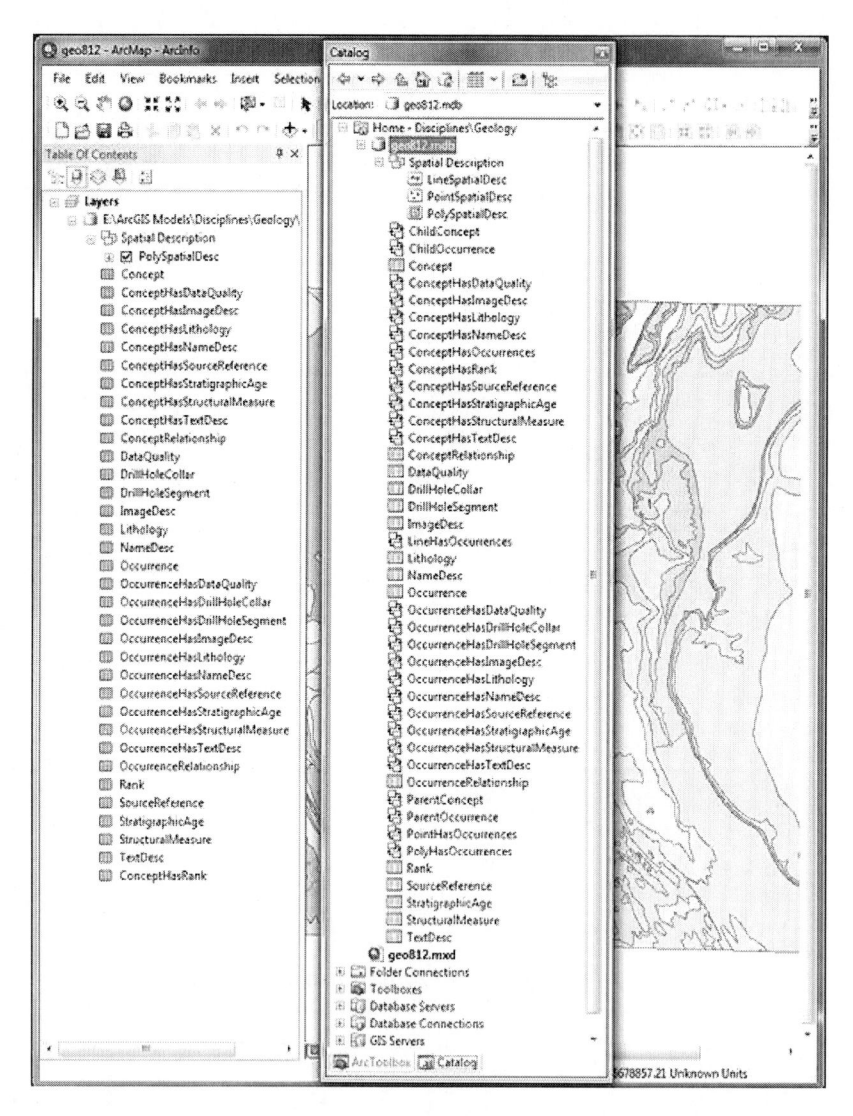

Figure 4. An example of a data model for geological mapping in the catalog window complemented by the ArcGIS project in the background (http://support.esri.com/en/downloads/datamodel/detail/30, July 25th 2012).

4. DATA MANAGEMENT AND SEMANTIC WEB

The need for geospatial reasoning has significantly increased in many software applications ranging from personal mobile tools, web search applications and local aware mobile services, to specialized systems such as emergency services, environmental monitoring systems or spatial web based browsers.

In response to required advanced information processing capabilities, the field of geospatial semantics has emerged as a new domain in the recent years. It becomes the area that focuses on the semantics aspect in geo-spatial information science, and deals with knowledge driven or intelligent processing techniques. The domain of geospatial semantics originates three separate areas such as geo-spatial information processing, semantic web technologies, and rapidly increasing use of location-aware mobile systems and similar devices [11].

In order to realize remote data management and sematic webs, GIS servers were developed to transform map layers, imagery, data, and GIS tools to desktop GIS, mobile devices and web based applications. In additions to the data management of raster and vector formats, a few web based services are used to support semantic webs. A Web Map Service (WMS) represents widely used a standard protocol for serving map images that are generated by a server using spatial data from a database. The first WMS protocol was developed by Open Geospatial Consortium (OGC) in 1999 (http://www.opengeospatial.org/standards, July 25th 2012). Other protocols often implemented in web based applications are the Web Feature Service (WCS) for dealing with feature description, andthe Web Map Tile Service (WMTS) for sharing map image tiles.

Many other standards have been developed in order to support semantic web systems such as the Web Processing Service (WPS), the Web Coverage Service (WCS), and the Web Coverage Processing Service (WCPS). As the interface standards, they provide rules for inputs and outputs in the framework of geospatial processing services. The OGC standards are mostly depended on a generalized architecture that is captured in a set of documents collectively designated as the Abstract Specification. It describes a basic data model for representing geographic features. The relationship between clients/servers and OGC protocols is illustrated in Figure 5.

A few server technologies are used on the Internet. Generally, the GIS servers can be divided into open source platforms and commercial systems. The MapServer represents an open source platform.

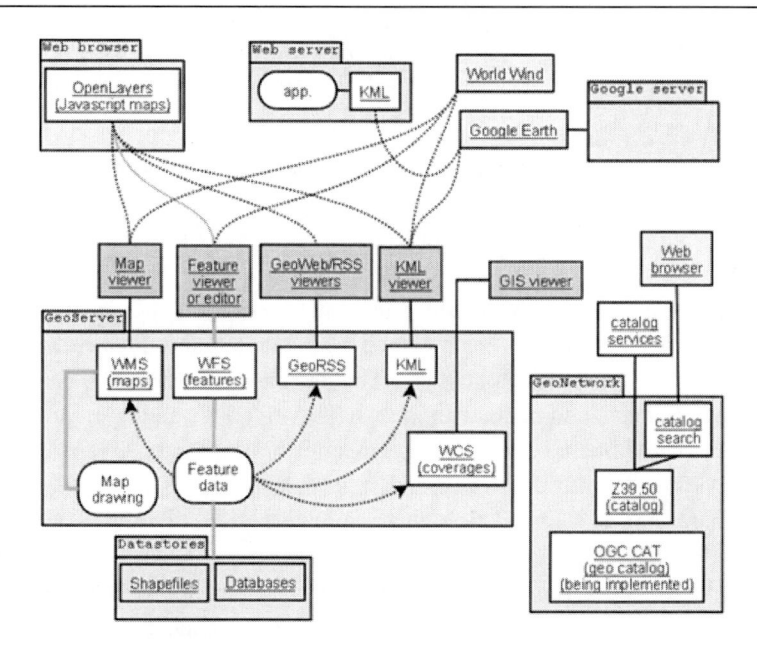

Figure 5. The relationship between clients/servers and OGC protocols
(http://www.opengeospatial.org/standards, July 25th 2012).

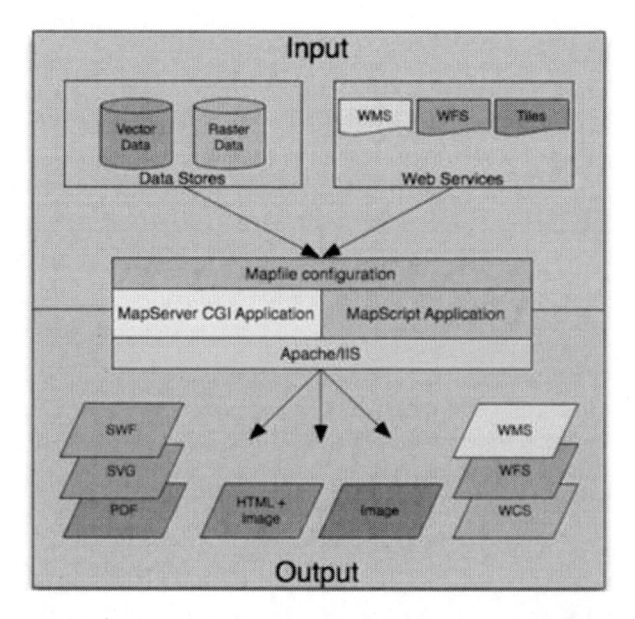

Figure 6. The basic architecture of the MapServerapplications managing data stores and web services (http://mapserver.org/introduction.html#introduction, July 25th 2012).

It is a widely used GIS server for publishing geo-spatial data and interactive mapping applications to the web, Figure 6 [12]. It supports display and querying of many raster, vector and database formats and can manage web mapping services such as WMS, WFS and WMTS. Basic MapServer configuration concepts focused on using vector and raster data, projection and labeling, layer and class ordering are described in tutorials that include many examples on how to use HTML templates to manage data via interactive web mapping applications [13].

The products such as ArcGIS Desktop, ArcGIS Engine, and ArcGIS Server represent commercial systems that are all built from ArcObjects, the collection of components for customization, extension and development of GIS applications [14]. Unlike ArcGIS Desktop and other ArcObjects local applications, clients of an ArcGIS Server access the ArcObjects components remotely. The ArcGIS Server manages map services, globe services, and geocode services mostly based on widely used standards. The GIS resources hosted on the ArcGIS server is used to be accessed through desktop applications such as ArcGIS Explorer, ArcGIS Desktop or other ArcObjects local applications. Also, developers can build own web applications that end users access through web browsers. The ArcGIS Server allows to create services that are enabled for access over web. The WMS, WFS, WCS, as well as Keyhole Markup Language (KML) services are availablein addition to built-in functionality for creation of map, geocode, globe, geodata, geoprocessing, mobile data and network web services. The workflow for making of geographic information available through the ArcGIS server includes three steps based on authoring the GIS resources using desktop GIS applications, publishing the resources as a service using ArcGIS server, and using the service through a client application, Figure 7. The ArcGIS Sever can be complemented by optional extensions that allow to create applications leveraging advanced features. Widely used extensions include the 3D extension (creation and analyzing surfaces such as slope, aspects, and hillshade analysis), the ArcPad extension (authoring and publishing projects from mobile GIS,ArcPad, synchronizing data between ArcPad and ArcGIS server),the data interoperability extension (distribution of data in many formats), the image extension (processing large volumes of raster data in native formats and different projections, and resolutions), the network extension (network-based spatial analysis capabilities including routing, travel directions, closest facilities, and service area analysis), the spatial extension (creation and analysis of cell-based raster data). Like ESRI's desktop applications, the ArcGIS server is built on ArcObjects components that have multiple developer APIs. These include Component Object Model (COM), .NET, Java, and C++. The ArcGIS server providing the framework for running ArcObjects in a server environment offers to develop other case oriented projects. An example of the project using WMS for serving the images from a satellite scene is illustrated in Figure 8.

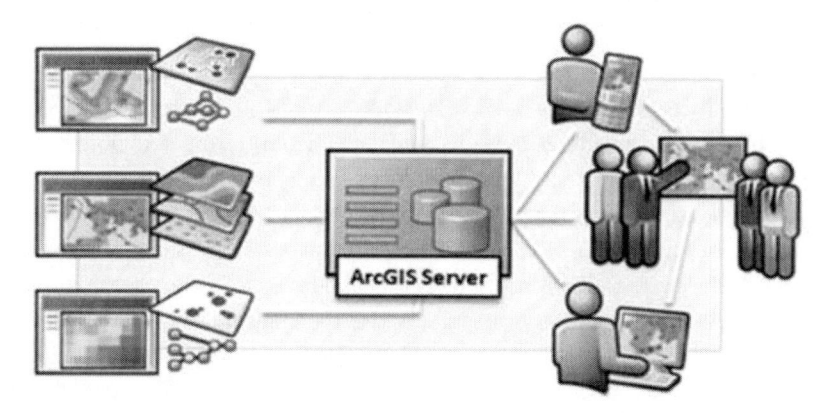

Figure 7. The workflow for making of geographic information available through the ArcGIS server (http://www.esri.com/software/arcgis/arcgisserver, July 25th 2012).

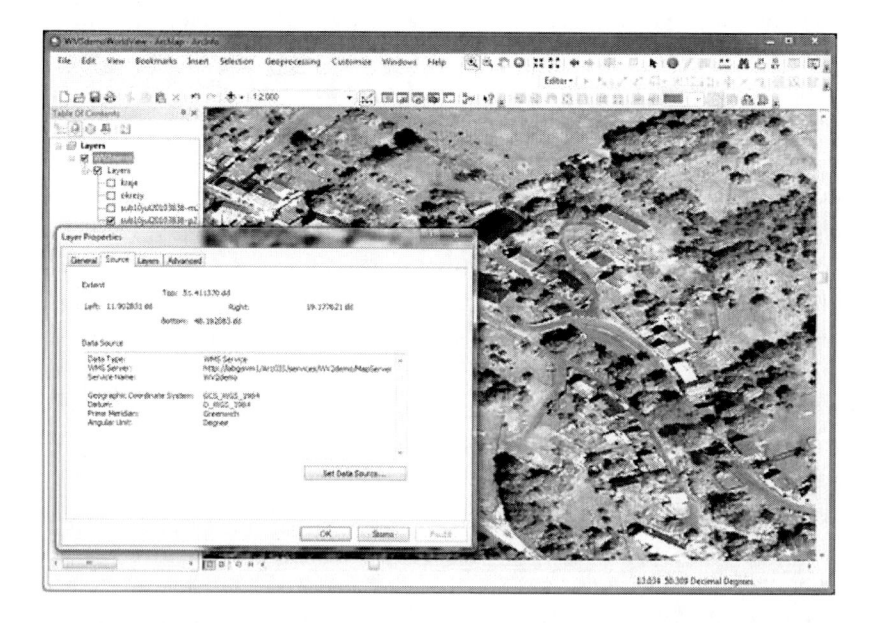

Figure 8. An example of the project using WMS for serving the images from a satellite scene.

5. DATA MANAGEMENT USING CLOUD COMPUTING TOOLS

Cloud computing is an emerging computing paradigm, which offers delivering data management services in a new way. Existing DBMSs and GISs together with semantic web technologies are taken into the sphere of interconnected data more accessible software tools, which rationalize the way they manage their resources. Moreover, data management tools are accessible for a wide range of participating users. It significantly simplifies the administration procedures, and reduces the upfront costs of computing. Thus, the cloud-based data management simplifies data storage and maintenance by providing a low-cost, scalable, location-independent platform. Data management tools based on cloud computing offer services to users worldwide. It also enables energy-efficient hosting of cloud applications from a wide range of domains. A potentially formidable risk for missing or corrupting data must be avoided by audit services that are critical to ensure the integrity and availability of outsourced data and to achieve credibility in cloud computing. However, data centers hosting cloud applications consume huge amounts of electrical energy, contributing to high operational costs [15, 16, 17]. The high rate at which stand data management tools changing places substantial pressures on organizational budgets. This situation will probably be made worse under the difficult economic conditions of some educational institutions. However, cloud computing can provide many of these institutions with an opportunity to continue to take advantages of new developments in recent DBMS, GIS and semantic web technologies at affordable costs. It is being recognized by a number of educational and research establishments. Many of them have found cloud computing to be attractive for use in their courses and research activities [18, 19, 20, 21].

6. DATA MANAGEMENT IN CLOUD COMPUTING: EXAMPLES

Cloud computing has a few key elements for its expansion into a vast topic that encompasses many different subjects in the framework of data management in the semantic web applications. It enables new web services by connecting users via networks that are constructed using multiple cloud services. New applications can be easier to create and can be based on standard modular parts. Users will be connected through the cloud wherever they are and at all times.

The attached case studies demonstrate the use of spatial data management tools based on GIS and other supporting technology. The projects were tested on a local network that can simulate running of applications in the cloud computing environment, Figure 9. The local network includesa set of virtual servers and a set of virtual workstations (Windows Server 2008 Hyper-V: 1 virtual Windows Server 2008 extended by WWW server, FTP server, SQL server, print server and ArcGIS server publishing data based on the case oriented studies; 1 virtual Windows Server 2008 extended by domain controller services; 8 virtual desktops running Windows 7 complemented by the application softwaresuch as ArcGIS desktop and other software tools). The projects are installed on virtual desktops and linked with data resources via web based services [22].

The first case study demonstrates spatial data management and sharingthe aerial photographs via WMS. The image of an ArcGIS user interface shows mapping of vegetation in the environment of the abandoned sedimentation basin of a former mining area, Figure 10.

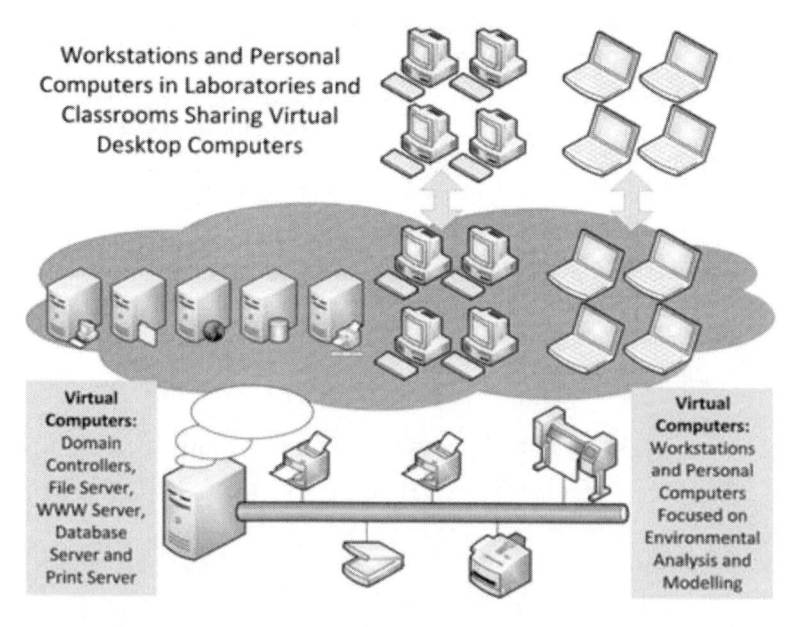

Figure 9. A set of virtual servers and virtual workstations based on Windows operating systems complemented by the ArcGIS server, the ArcGIS desktops, and case oriented studies focused on spatial data management and semantic web applications [23].

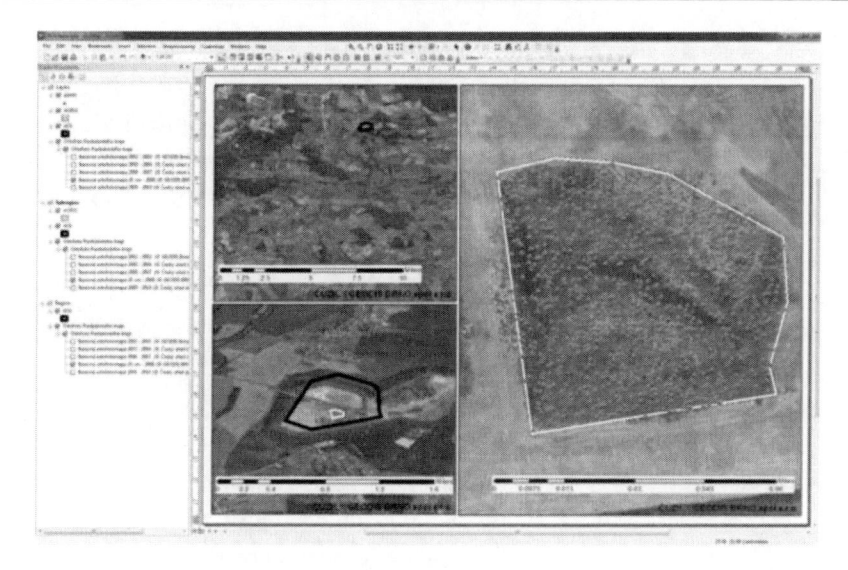

Figure 10. The image of an ArcGIS user interface that shows mapping of vegetation in the environment of the abandoned sedimentation basin of a former mining area in a few scales.

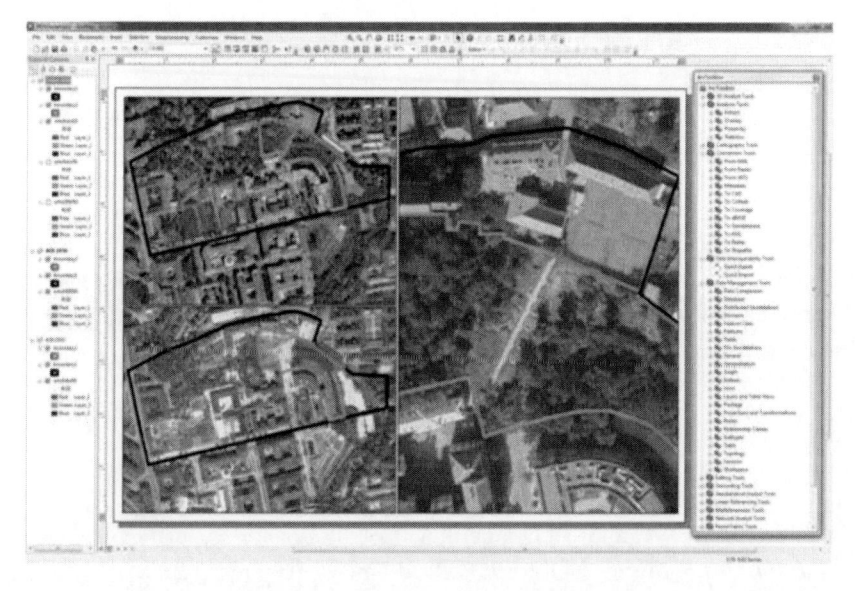

Figure 11. The image ofan ArcGIS user interface that showsthe land-cover changes in an approximate period of 50 years, and a part of the area of interest (AOI) in a higher resolution (on the right side).

The second case study deals with aerial photographs of the urban environment in various resolutions and time acquisition. The image of an ArcGIS user interface shows the land-cover changes in an approximate period of 50 years, Figure 11.

CONCLUSION

Presented research focused on data management, involving GIS and cloud computing, represents a new application domain that also outlines new means in the framework of the semantic web. It promises to provide opportunity for delivering a variety of computing services in a way that has not been experienced previously. Combining datamanagement services with new technologies such as GIS [24, 25, 26, 27], remote sensing [28, 29, 30], and global positioning system (GPS) [31, 32, 33] can bring new ways of exploration inthe decision-making processes that are dealing with data management and semantic web applications. The potential of data processing based on cloud computing for improving efficiency and cost has been also recognized for a few years of testing and using at universities and applied research institutions.

ACKNOWLEDGMENT

The presented research was carried out in the framework of the GIS Laboratory research projects supported by the Ministry of Education, Youth and Sports. Partial results were presented at the conference WORLDCOMP'11 in Las Vegas 2011, and at theAnnual Conference of the iEMSs in Leipzig 2012.

REFERENCES

[1] Burrough, P.A. and McDonnell, A. (1998). *Principles of Geographical Information Systems*. Oxford: Oxford University Press.
[2] Johnston, J.A. (1998). *Geographic Information Systems in Ecology*. London: Blackwell Science.

[3] Zeiler, M. (2010). *Modeling Our World: The ERSI Guide to Geodatabase Concepts*.2nd editions. Redlands, California: ESRI Press.
[4] Rigaux, P., Scholl, M. and Voisard, A. (2002). *Spatial Database with Application to GIS*.San Francisco: Morgan Kaufmann Publishers.
[5] Arctur, D. and Zeiler, M. (2004). *Designing Geodatabases: Case Studies in GIS Data Modeling*. Redlands, California: ESRI Press.
[6] MacDonald, A. (2001). *Building a Geodatabase*. Redlands, California: ESRI Press.
[7] Mitchell, A. (1999). *The ESRI Guide to GIS Analysis*. Volume 1: Geographic Patterns and Relationships. Redlands, California: ESRI Press.
[8] Mitchell, A. (2005). *The ESRI Guide to GIS Analysis*. Volume 2: Spatial Measurements and Statistics. Redlands, California: ESRI Press.
[9] Maguire, D.J., Batty, M. and Goodchild, M.F. (2005). *GIS, Spatial Analysis and Modeling*. Redlands, California: ESRI Press.
[10] Maidment, D.R. (2002). *Arc Hydro: GIS for Water Resources*. Redlands, California: ESRI Press.
[11] Ashish, N. and Sheth, A.P.P. (2011). *Semantic Web and Beyond: Computing for Human Experience, Geospatial Semantics and Semantic Web, Foundations, Algorithms, and Applications*. New York: Springer.
[12] McKenna, J., Fawcett, D. and Butler, H. (2012). *An Introduction to MapServer*. http://mapserver.org/introduction.html#introduction, July 25th 2012.
[13] Nacionales, P.S. and McKenna, J. (2012). *MapServer Tutorial*. http:// mapserver.org/tutorial/index.html, July 25th 2012.
[14] Burke, R. (2003). *Getting to Know ArcObjects: Programming ArcGIS with VBA*. Redlands, California: ESRI Press.
[15] Sosinsky, B. (2011). *Cloud Computing Bible*. Indianapolis: Wiley.
[16] Jamsa, K. (2012). *Cloud Computing*. Burlington: Jones and Bartlett Learning.
[17] Rhoton, J. (2011). *Cloud Computing: Implementation Handbook for Enterprises*. United Kingdom: Recursive Press.
[18] Zissis, D. and Lekkas, D. (2012). Addressing cloud computing security issues. *Future Generation Computer Systems 28*, 583-592.
[19] Marston, S., Li, Z., Bandyopadhyay, S., Zhang, J. and Ghalsasi, A. (2011). Cloud computing-The business perspective. *Decision Support Systems 51*, 176-189.
[20] Sultan, N. (2010). Cloud computing for education? *International Journal of Information Management 30*, 109-116.

[21] Ercan, T. (2010). Effective use of cloud computing in educational institutions. *Procedia Social and Behavioral Sciences2*, 938-942.
[22] Matejicek, L. (2011). GIS Laboratory: New Trends in Research and Education in Environmental Science Based on Advanced Computing Tools. In: H.R. Arabnia, V.A. Clincy, L. Deligiannidis (Eds.) *Proceedings of the 2011 International Conference on Frontiers in Education: Computer Science and Computer Engineering (FECS 2011)*. WORLDCOMP'11, Las Vegas, Nevada, USA, July 2011.
[23] Matejicek, L. (2012). Environmental Modelling Using Cloud Computing Tools: Case Studies and Examples. In: R. Seppelt, A.A. Voinov, S. Lange, D. Bankamp (Eds.) *Proceedings of the International Environmental Modelling and Software Society (iEMSs) 2012, International Congress on Environmental Modelling and Software Managing Resources of a Limited Planet*. Leipzig, Germany, July 2012.
[24] Goodchild, M.F., Steyaert, L.T. and Parks, B.O. (1996). *GIS and Environmental Modeling: Progress and Research Issues*. Fort Collins: GIS World, Inc.
[25] Cromley, E.K. and McLafferty, S.L. (2002). *GIS and Public Health*. New York: The Guilford Press.
[26] Martin, D. (1996). *Geographic Information Systems: Socioeconomic applications*. New York: Routledge.
[27] Matejicek, L. (2011). *Environmental Modeling with GIS*. New York: Nova Science Publishers.
[28] Paine, D.P. and Kiser, J.D. (2003). *Aerial Photography and Image Interpretation*. 2nd edition. New York: Wiley.
[29] Shunlin, L. (2004). *Quantitative remote sensing of land surfaces*. New Jersey: Wiley.
[30] Blaschke, T. (2010). Object-based image analysis for remote sensing. *ISPRS Journal of Photogrammetry and Remote Sensing 65*, 2-16.
[31] Grewal, M.S., Weill, L.R. and Andrews, A.P. (2001). *Global Positioning Systems, Inertial Navigation, and Integration*. New York: Wiley.
[32] Matejicek, L. (2003). Development of Software Tools for Ecological Field Studies Using ArcPad. http://gis.esri.com/library/userconf/proc03/p0333.pdf, July 25th 2012.
[33] Matejicek, L. (2010). *Environmental Modeling with GPS*. New York: Nova Science Publishers.

In: Data Security, Data Mining ...
Editor: Serge O'Byrne

ISBN: 978-1-62417-582-4
© 2013 Nova Science Publishers, Inc.

Chapter 4

NOTHING HAPPENS UNTIL IT HAPPENS

Mads Ronald Dahl and Eivind Ortind Simonsen
Aarhus University, Center for Medical Education, Denmark

ABSTRACT

Usage of information technology and communication (ICT) is of fundamental importance to the daily operation of the modern organization.

Data security is a chimera in many forms and the on-going production, sharing and storage of knowledge, information and big data have to be robust to withstand the constant development of the digital environment and architecture. Information technology (IT) is used to control and distribute general information, personal data, and highly classified and sensitive data. As part of the university development, we have implemented several learning management systems (LMS) used by the administration, teachers, and students. The LMS has become a central part of the university ICT portfolio and provide the opportunities for effective and flexible teaching and learning environments. One set of challenges is to guide and educate the users of the systems in general data security issues, on one side, and keep the system aligned to security standards on the system administration side. These two stakeholders have completely different views and expectations to the system and they operate either frontend (users) or backend (system administration). Thus, a potential misinterpretation of needs can lead to a breach in data security. Furthermore, the organization, IT policy, and standards need more than text, intentions, and publication: it must be pushed and supported to achieve awareness of increased data security.

Digital identification and authentication often relay on unique usernames and passwords. In Denmark every citizen has a unique personal identification number (CPR-number) used for any communication with public services, such as local and national government, education, healthcare, etc. Also, the ID is being used for identification in the private sector, such as banking, renting, and memberships. This widespread usage of the CPR-number makes it the single most important number to any individual.

In this paper we will illustrate how fragile data security can be when the system architecture, authorization, and validation are founded on a personal identification number (PIN). We tested the automated support systems, where requests for forgotten passwords and account reset options were possible. These systems are often services, such as mail account, cloud computers, LMS, or intranet elements. Since the user identification for these systems could be based on the unique CPR number, chances are that this information can be extracted. In conclusion, we urge not to use CPR, social security number, and comparable numbers as identification key for general systems. These numbers are personal and should only be used for registration in administration system with no public access and the highest standard of data security.

INTRODUCTION

Data Security requires proactive management, an in depth understanding of the actual technological infrastructure and architecture, and an informed organization that complies with good data practice [1-3]. Workflow within the modern digitalized knowledge organization is complex and ever more dependent on stable and secure information technology and a competent workforce [4].

Making a secure network inside a complex organization is no trivial task, since the components are inhomogeneous and unmixable ingredients. At one end we have the strict mathematics and computer science of algorithms, cryptography, equations and logic while at the other end sits the users who are multitasking, by-passing, exchanging and producing. [5].

For complete control there would have to be a dynamic list of all hardware, mobile technologies, software, networks, systems, and actions taken, which is utopia. Therefore, no system will ever be perfect or completely secure, and the technical department is in a dilemma of restricting the systems and at the same time optimizing the workflow [5]. Administration will have access to data that can often be classified as Big Data, but the individual administrator seldom distinguishes in a qualified manner regarding specific types of content. Data gathered, stored, accessed, analyzed, and used must meet the highest standard, so the servants have got to understand the importance of the role they play in the workflow and the responsibility they hold [6].

The individual users of data and technology are dependent on a range of permissions, usernames, and passwords to conduct their daily work. The user access to organization data is often administrated using a role based control model or Role-based access control (RBAC) [7]. Thus, in theory and on paper, the implementation of these standards should ensure data security and prevent data losses using technology through good management and a clear policy. However, it is evident that classified data and vital information are being exposed at any time through e.g. online presentations [8], publicly available documents [9], and via the general info sphere [10].

In Denmark every citizen is given an identification number at birth for the Central Population Registry (CPR). The CPR number is unique and personal and can never be changed or reused; thus, CPR number is an unambiguous identification of one – and only one – person [11]. The number consists of 10 digits: the first six correspond to the date of birth (day, month, and year, two digits each), followed by a four digit serial number. This serial number is generated by an algorithm that verifies whether the number is genuine, gives the century of birth, and identifies the person's gender (even numbers are assigned to women). For example, the (fictive) number 121056–1234 refers to a woman born on 12 October 1956.

At present, the CPR number is practically the data index key for authorization to all public services and registrations (ref). Furthermore the number is essential for the success of research conducted on the various Danish registry databases enabling comparison on an individual basis [12].

The entire Danish population can be identified on an individual level using information from public registries with data, such as date of birth, gender, name, place of birth, citizenship, identity of parents, and continuously updated information on vital status, place of residence and spouses [13, 14]. It has even been described as 'the entire country is a cohort' [15]. The meticulous registration of the population has given research a wealth of data to work with. The CPR number is to be considered as confidential personal information, and all relevant research has to be approved by the Danish Data Protection Agency [16].

Due to the strength of the CPR number as a unique identification key it has been exploited and implemented as an unique identification in databases ranging from bank accounts to video and sport clubs.

Data loss can be anything from devastating to inconsequential. Losing the CPR number to the wrong people can be the beginning of a troubling occurrence of identity theft. This type of crime is on the rise at an alarming rate worldwide with more than 11 million adult victims in the US alone costing billions of dollars and personal costs [17].

Another problem is when criminals succeed in obtaining personal digital information and subsequently misuse it for own benefits, economical, simple hacking vandalism, or reputation.

MATERIALS AND METHOD

The university is a modern organization with a wide spread usage of information and communication technology (ICT), computers, mail and web servers, cloud computing, web, Learning management systems (LMS), and much more. The initial observation of a potential data security risk was a serendipity result of a system architecture investigation.

This study was conducted on the administrative non-encrypted internet services of a university organization with currently more than 40.000 students and 10.000 employees in Denmark. The first investigation was in 2010 and subsequently with approximately two months intervals. One of the services tested was the main learning management system provided by the University to all students and teachers. The main LMS was an Open Source Software offering a virtual learning environment, as a client/server web application. Open source LMS, such as Moodle, Ilias, eduplone, Claroline, SAKAI, WebCT, and Bscware are extensively implemented at universities worldwide [18].

To access the LMS users have to enter either a username and password or request for access using a pin code in combination with the Danish CPR-number. Non-Danish citizen can request for a CPR-like identification number that after registration can be used.

The LMS "new user/forgotten password" feature was submitted to our security test, since it was an exclusive client to system server communication involving a database containing the personal CPR number. On entering our own CPR numbers in the forgotten password service we received a detailed auto reply from the server.

We made the administration aware of the security issue several times before a patch was implemented to solve the problem. Due to system maintenance, updates, or oblivion the patch did not follow the development and within 6 months the old issue re-emerged. This time we tried to follow the University security policy and documented our findings.

RESULTS

When we tested the system, we used a combination of numbers we knew existed, and numbers we knew did not exist. Depending on which number we used, we would get a reply from the system stating, that this number is either not found in our system, or an email has been sent to the email address, so that the password can be reset.

Positive result on valid CPR nr.:

- E-mail with activation link sent by noreply@dk.dk: mads_dahl@mail.dk

If we received this email reply we knew, that a person with this CPR number (and this email address) was connected to this institution.

Negative result on non-valid CPR nr.:

- Illegal user-ID - must start with your date of birth, as ddmmyy and have a length of 10 characters.

If we received this email reply we knew, that no person with this CPR number was connected to this institution.

This made us wonder whether it would be possible to figure out all the CPR numbers of random students and employees at this institution, just by going through the range of CPR numbers.

If the 10 digit CPR number was a random number, this would be a laborious task, because we would have to make 10.000.000.000 requests. However, we know that the CPR numbers are not random. The first four digits have to represent a day and a month, so there are only 500 valid combinations, in contrast to the 10.000 random combinations that are possible with four digits. Digits number five and six have to represent a year, and although there are 100 possible combinations, we know that persons affiliated with a university – especially students – will most likely be of a certain age.

The last four digits represent a control number. If this was a random number, there would again be 10.000 possible combinations. However, this number is not random. The control number has to adhere to a Modulo 11 test reducing the possible control numbers to roughly 540 numbers. By exploiting this knowledge, we were able to reduce the amount of total requests we had to make.

We made a program using Java, where tailor made HTTP requests were sent to the website, and the responses were stored in two arrays, denoting either success or failure. The website had a built-in control feature that tested for IP addresses. This meant that the website would only allow one request per hour from a certain IP address. By spoofing IP addresses we were able to circumvent this control feature, and complete the requests within two hours. The array with successful requests contained both CPR numbers and the email address associated to that CPR address.

The program was thought of as a proof-of-concept, and the information we gained wasn't used. We did not want to collect any of the potential personal information on anyone who was oblivious to the issue. Thus we only tested further on five informed individuals.

The results were presented to the IT department who after a while made a new autoreply patch stating:

- E-mail with activation link sent by noreply@dk.dk

Negative result on non-valid CPR nr.:

- Illegal user-ID - must start with your date of birth as ddmmyy and have a length of 10 characters.

After a period of more than six months the LMS was updated without the patch. Thus, the autoreply again contained the email address.

Even the solution with the patch gave away information on the database, since the reply effectively confirmed the validity of a given CPR nr.

DISCUSSION AND CONCLUSION

The coupling of CPR number and email address makes it relatively easy to discover, whom the CPR number belongs to. While the CPR number is anonymous, apart from gender and age, the email address seldom is. Often it is a matter of making a simple search on the Internet to discover the name of the person associated to an email address. You might even discover the address of that person utilizing certain web services. With the information of name, address, and CPR number a malicious person can relatively easily make an identity theft.

The recent case of Mat Honan [19], tragic as it was, confined itself to his digital identity. The cases of misuse of CPR numbers in Denmark have to do with real life identity. Mostly, the identity theft facilitated by using another person's CPR number has to do with financial gains, but there are also examples of people getting prescription medicine in the name of another person.

The exploitation of real life identity of individual persons in Denmark, and the exploitation of the digital identity of Mat Honan, were made possible, because persons situated in a large organization didn't realize, that they were giving important information away. Whether it is the last four digits on a credit card or an email address, these small tidbits are often more than enough to wreak havoc. For Mat Honan, changing his email address might be enough to ensure that the exploitation of his digital identity does not happen again. Unfortunately, the Danish victims of identity theft are not that lucky. You cannot just change your CPR number, and therefore the exploitation could, in theory, continue for your entire life time.

Therefore, it is of vital importance that the usage of a CPR numbers is kept at a minimum. If an organization deems it absolutely necessary to use CPR numbers, that organization should deploy stringent procedures to ensure, that no other information is associated to the CPR number, thereby making the possibility of identity theft more difficult than a simple web search.

REFERENCES

[1] Stoneburner G, Goguen A, Feringa A (2002). *Risk management guide for information technology systems.* National Institute of Standards and Technology Special Publication,800(30).

[2] Brancheau JC, Janz BD, Wetherbe JC (1996). "Key Issues in Information Systems Management: 1994-95 SIM Delphi Results," *MIS Quarterly* 20:2;225-242.

[3] Petter S, DeLone W, McLean ER (2012). "The Past, Present, and Future of "IS Success"," *Journal of the Association for Information Systems:* 13(5,2).

[4] Eardley T. NHS Informatics Workforce Survey (2006). *ASSIST:* London, England.
[5] Schneier B (2000). Secrets and Lies. *Digital Security in a Networked World.* John Wiley and Sons, Inc., 1 edition.
[6] Wind-Cowie M, Lekhi R (2012). *The data dividend.* Demos, London, England.
[7] Sandhu R, Coyne EJ, Feinstein HL, Youman CE (1996). *Role-based access control models IEEE Computer,* 29:38–47.
[8] Dahl MR, Høyer CB. Professional PowerPoint presentations can compromise data security (2009). *J. Inform. Ass. Sec.* 4:42–47.
[9] Dahl MR, Simonsen EO, Høyer CB.
[10] O'Hara K. (2012). Data Quality, Government Data and the Open Data Infosphere. *AISB/IACAP World Congress 2012: Information Quality Symposium,* Birmingham, GB.
[11] Central Office of Civil Registration. *The Civil Registration System in Denmark.* Webpage 27 September 2001, accessed 11 July 2012.
[12] Hallas J (2001). Conducting pharmacoepidemiologic research in Denmark. *J. Pharmacoepi. Drug Safety* 10: 619–623.
[13] Mortensen PB (2004). Registerforskning i Danmark. *Norsk. Epidemiologi* 14(1):21–124.
[14] Pedersen CB. The Danish Civil Registration System (2011). *Scand. J. Public Health.* 39(7):(suppl)22-25.
[15] Frank L (2000). Epidemiology: when an entire country is a cohort. *Science* 287:2398–2399.
[16] The Act on Processing of Personal Data (Act No. 429 of 31 May 2000). *Introduction to the Danish Data Protection Agency.* Webpage from 26 august 2010, accessed 04 July 2012.
[17] Miceli D and Kim R (2010) *Identity Fraud Survey Report.* Javelin Strategy and Research 1:21.
[18] Sabine G and Beate L. (2005) "An Evaluation of Open Source e-learning Platforms Stressing Adaptation Issues", in: *Proceedings of Fifth IEEE International Conference on Learning Technologies,* IEEE, Ischia, Italy.
[19] Honan M (2012) http://www.wired.com/gadgetlab/2012/08/apple-amazon-mat-honan-hacking/.

INDEX

#

21st century, 35

A

abstraction, 50, 51
access, x, 12, 20, 22, 24, 25, 51, 59, 68, 69, 70, 74
accessibility, 42
acid, 8, 26, 27
adaptations, ix, 32, 40
adenine, 5
advanced data management, ix, 49
age, 71, 72
agriculture, 36
algorithm, vii, 2, 5, 16, 17, 21, 23, 26, 29, 44, 69
amino, 7, 10, 27
amino acid(s), 7, 10, 27
annotation, viii, 32, 36, 37, 38, 39, 41, 45, 46, 53
aquaculture, 36, 45
arginine, 10
artificial intelligence, 33
assessment, 3
assets, ix, 49
atmospheric pressure, 27
atoms, 10
audit, 61

authentication, x, 68
awareness, x, 67

B

banking, x, 51, 68
base, 6, 7, 8, 9, 10, 11, 12, 24, 40
base pair, 6, 9
benefits, 70
bias, 34
Bible, 65
biochemistry, viii, 32
bioinformatics, 33, 34, 35, 37, 38, 39
biological processes, 39
biological responses, viii, 32, 43
biological systems, 8
biomarkers, 43
biosensors, ix, 32, 39
biotechnology, 44, 45, 46
bonds, 5, 7, 8
Brazil, 31
browser, 34

C

C++, 60
CAD, 53
calculus, 52
campaigns, 42
cancer, 2, 4, 37

carbon, 4, 16, 22, 25
carcinogenesis, vii, 1
case study(s), 54, 62, 64
cation, 8
cell cycle, 2
cell death, vii, 1, 3, 4
challenges, vii, x, 34, 42, 46, 67
chemical, 9, 10, 12, 14, 20, 22, 24, 25, 38, 47
chemical reactions, 24
chemical structures, 24
chimera, ix, 67
chromosome, 4, 26, 29
cities, 53
citizenship, 69
classes, 5, 54
classification, 33, 34, 39
clients, 57, 58, 59
cloud computing, 61, 65
clustering, vii, viii, 2, 5, 16, 20, 22, 23, 26, 29, 33, 34
clusters, vii, 2, 5, 11, 16, 17, 18, 20, 22
coding, 36
collaboration, 44
commercial, 53, 57, 59
communication, ix, x, 45, 67, 68, 70
compaction, 8
complement, 53
complex lesions, vii, 2, 16
complexity, 2, 9, 12, 16
composition, 10, 27
compounds, 43
computer, 33, 43, 44, 51, 68
computing, viii, ix, 2, 5, 11, 16, 20, 22, 23, 49, 50, 53, 61, 62, 64, 65, 66, 70
conference, 64
configuration, 4, 5, 16, 17, 22, 59
Congress, 66, 74
constituents, 10
construction, 37
contour, 50
correlation(s), 10, 32, 36
cost, 25, 32, 36, 61, 64
CPU, 20, 23
criminals, 70

cryptography, 68
cytosine, 5
Czech Republic, 49

D

damages, vii, 1, 2, 4, 9, 10, 21, 22, 24
data analysis, 35, 40, 43
data center, 61
data distribution, 43
data mining, vii, viii, 5, 15, 24, 31, 32, 33, 34, 35, 36, 37, 40, 41, 42, 43, 44, 45, 46, 47
data processing, 64
data set, 33, 35, 42, 43
data structure, 51
data transfer, 23
database, viii, 2, 32, 33, 34, 35, 39, 51, 53, 57, 59, 70, 72
database management, 51, 53
decay, 8
decision-making process, ix, 49, 64
Denmark, x, 67, 68, 69, 70, 73, 74
Density Based Spatial Clustering Algorithm with Noise (DBSCAN), viii, 2
deoxyribonucleic acid, 2
deoxyribose, 5, 7, 26
deposition, vii, 1, 2, 3, 16, 18, 20, 23, 24, 25
deposits, 3, 4, 11, 15, 22
depth, 13, 68
detection, 10, 32, 40, 47
diffusion, 13, 15, 25
direct action, 8
discriminant analysis, 33
dispersion, 50
dissociation, 8
distribution, 4, 9, 11, 13, 14, 15, 22, 45, 59
DNA, v, vii, viii, 1, 2, 3, 4, 5, 6, 7, 8, 9, 10, 12, 14, 15, 16, 17, 19, 20, 22, 24, 25, 26, 34, 35, 45, 46
DNA damage, vii, viii, 1, 2, 5, 8, 10, 12, 16, 20, 24, 25
DNA strand breaks, 20
double helix, 4, 5
drug discovery, 40, 42

drug targets, 40
drugs, 40

E

economics, viii, 31
education, ix, x, 50, 65, 68
educational institutions, 61, 66
e-learning, 74
electromagnetic, 25
electron(s), 3, 4, 8, 11, 12, 15, 16, 18, 19, 20, 21, 26, 28, 29
electrophoresis, 10, 18
elucidation, 35, 37
emergency, 57
employees, 70, 71
energy, vii, 1, 2, 3, 4, 9, 11, 12, 15, 16, 17, 18, 20, 22, 23, 24, 25, 26, 28, 29, 61
energy transfer, 3, 11, 18
engineering, viii, 31
England, 46, 47, 74
environment(s), ix, 8, 32, 40, 45, 50, 51, 52, 53, 60, 62, 63, 64, 67
enzymatic activity, 39
enzyme(s), viii, 32, 34, 36, 37, 39
enzyme inhibitors, viii, 32
EST, viii, 32, 36, 37, 46, 47
eukaryotic, 5, 7
eukaryotic cell, 7
Europe, 34
evolution, 45
excitation, 15, 18, 20
execution, ix, 49
experimental design, 35
expertise, 42, 44
exploitation, 73
exposure, 10
expressed sequence tag(s) (ESTs), viii, 31, 36, 44, 45, 46, 47
extraction, 44, 53

F

fibers, 10

financial, 32, 73
financial institutions, 32
fish, 45
fitness, 36
flexibility, 44
fluctuations, 42
force, 10
formation, 8, 9, 11, 27, 29
fragments, 16
fraud, 32
free radicals, 8, 14, 15, 25

G

gel, 10, 18
gene expression, 35, 40, 41, 42, 43, 47
genes, 34, 37, 38, 40, 41, 45
genetic code, 7
genetic diversity, 38
genetic information, 5
genetics, viii, 27, 32, 45, 46
genome, viii, 31, 34, 35, 36, 37, 38, 41, 45, 46
genomics, 34, 36, 39, 40, 41, 44, 45, 46
genotype, 37
Geographic Information System (GIS), ix, 49, 50, 51, 53, 54, 57, 59, 61, 62, 64, 66
geometry, 4, 22, 25, 53
Germany, 66
glycine, 10
GPS, 64, 66
growth, 33, 34, 36, 37, 40
guanine, 5

H

hacking, 70, 74
health, 41
helium, 28
heredity, 5
histone(s), 7
homeostasis, viii, 32
human body, 3
hydrogen, 5, 8

Index

hydrogen bonds, 5
hydrogen peroxide, 8
hydroxyl, 8
hypothesis, 35

I

ID, x, 68, 71, 72
identification, vii, viii, x, 32, 36, 37, 38, 39, 68, 69, 70
identity, 69, 70, 73
image(s), ix, 49, 50, 53, 57, 59, 60, 62, 63, 64, 66
image analysis, 66
imagery, 57
improvements, 37
independence, 51
individuals, 72
induction, 12, 15, 18
information processing, 57
information technology, ix, 67, 68, 73
infrastructure, 68
ingredients, 68
insertion, 40
institutions, 61
integration, 34, 40, 43
integrity, 53, 54, 61
interface, 53, 57, 62, 63, 64
interoperability, 59
interpretability, 38
ionization, 8, 12, 15, 17, 18, 20, 27, 28, 29
ions, viii, 2, 4, 12, 15, 16, 20, 22, 23, 25, 28, 29
IP address, 72
iron, 4, 22, 23
irradiation, 3, 4, 8, 10, 11, 12, 16, 22, 26

J

Japan, 28, 34
Java, 60, 72

K

Keynes, 1
kill, 13
Knowledge Discovery in Databases (KDD), viii, 31

L

labeling, 59
languages, 51
lead, vii, x, 1, 2, 4, 7, 8, 12, 32, 67
learning, ix, 33, 37, 67, 70
learning environment, x, 67, 70
learning management systems (LMS), ix, 67
Lebanon, 1
lesions, vii, 2, 8, 16, 24
linear model, 37
living cells, vii, 1, 16, 26
loci, viii, 32, 36, 37, 38, 46

M

machine learning, 33, 37
magnitude, 41
majority, 16
malignant tissues, 8
management, vii, ix, 33, 42, 45, 49, 50, 51, 52, 53, 54, 57, 61, 62, 64, 67, 68, 69, 70, 73
manipulation, 51
mapping, viii, 32, 40, 54, 56, 59, 62, 63
market segment, 32
marketing, 32
MAS, 36
mass, 3, 8, 20
mathematics, 68
matrix, 10
matter, 2, 4, 24, 43, 73
measurement(s), 4, 11, 27, 41
media, 28
medical, 2, 3
medicine, viii, 31, 36, 45, 73
memory, 24

Index

meta-analysis, 36, 40
metabolism, 36, 39
methodology, 4, 32, 38, 42
Mexico, 46
micrometer, 4
microsatellites, viii, 31, 36
Microsoft, 56
Ministry of Education, 64
mission, 2
misuse, 70, 73
mobile device, 57
models, ix, 12, 16, 25, 26, 29, 33, 34, 35, 41, 50, 51, 53, 54, 74
modifications, vii, 1, 2, 8, 9
molecular biology, viii, 31, 32, 34, 35
molecules, vii, 1, 4, 5, 8, 9, 10, 39
motif, 34, 41
multidimensional, 46
mutation(s), vii, 1, 2, 3, 4, 9

N

nanometers, 11
NHS, 74
nitrogen, 27
nuclei, 8
nucleic acid, 26, 27
nucleotide sequence, 34
nucleotides, 7
nucleus, 3, 4, 11, 25
null, 21
numerical analysis, 23
nutrient, 8
nutrition, 36

O

Open Geospatial Consortium (OGC), ix, 50, 57
operating system, 62
operations, 11, 51, 53
opportunities, ix, x, 50, 67
optimization, 29, 43
organic matter, 8

organism, 4, 34, 38
overlay, 53
oxidative damage, 8
oxygen, 8

P

Pacific, 45, 46
pairing, 6
Panama, 46
parallel, 4, 23
parallel processing, 23
parents, 5, 69
password, 70, 71
pathways, 34, 35, 37, 38, 39, 40, 41, 43
pattern recognition, viii, 31
personal computers, 50
pests, 37
phenotype(s), ix, 32, 37, 39, 42, 43
phosphate, 5, 7, 9
photoelectron spectroscopy, 27
photographs, ix, 49, 51, 62, 64
photons, 15, 25
physical interaction, 15, 22, 37, 40
physicians, 42
physics, 36
physiology, 38, 47
pipeline, 42
plants, viii, 31, 38
plasmid, 18, 22
plasmid DNA, 18, 22
platform, 34, 46, 57, 61
policy, x, 67, 69, 71
pollutants, 50
polyacrylamide, 10
polymer(s), 5, 10
polymorphism(s), viii, 31, 32, 36, 47
population, 34, 38, 40, 69
portfolio, ix, 67
preparation, 42
private sector, x, 68
probability, vii, 2, 9, 15, 17, 18, 21
productivity rates, 37
programming, 5, 23, 51, 56
programming languages, 23, 52

project, 34, 42, 54, 55, 56, 60
propane, 11, 27
protein codified, viii, 32
protein sequence, 34, 35, 38
proteins, 7, 8, 38, 39, 40
proteomics, 41, 44
protons, viii, 2, 4, 12, 13, 15, 16, 18, 20, 22, 23, 24, 26, 28, 29
public service, x, 68, 69
publishing, 59, 62
purines, 5, 6

Q

quality control, 32, 37, 43
quantitative trait loci (QTL), viii, 32, 36
query, viii, 32, 34, 50, 52

R

radiation, vii, 1, 2, 3, 5, 8, 9, 10, 11, 15, 16, 20, 22, 24, 26, 27, 28, 29
radiation damage, 24
radicals, 8, 9, 14, 27
radio, vii, 1, 2, 3, 20, 24
radiobiology, vii, viii, 1, 2, 5, 12, 17, 20, 24
radioprotection, vii, 1, 2
radiotherapy, vii, 1, 2, 29
radius, 22
reactions, 3, 8, 16, 39
reality, 11
reasoning, 57
recombination, 9
registry(s), 69
regression, 33, 41
regression analysis, 33, 41
relational model(s), 53
relevance, 38
remote sensing, 64, 66
repair, vii, 1, 2, 3, 4, 9, 27
repetitions, 7
reproduction, 5
reputation, 70
requirements, 22, 51

research activities, vii, 1, 61
research institutions, 64
researchers, 44
resistance, 36
resolution, 11, 63
resources, 39, 43, 59, 61, 62
response, 57
revenue, 32
ribonucleic acid, 5
risk, 61, 70
RNA, 5, 6, 34, 35
root, 22
rules, 44, 51, 53, 54, 57

S

salmon, 27
scaling, 28
scattering, 28, 29
schema, 35, 38
science, 2, 33, 44, 57, 68
scope, 8, 12
second generation, 53
security, vii, ix, x, 65, 67, 68, 69, 70, 71, 74
sedimentation, 62, 63
semantics, 57
sequencing, 36
servers, 57, 58, 62, 70
services, ix, x, 49, 57, 59, 61, 62, 64, 68, 70
shape, 18, 22
shoot, 17
shrimp, viii, 31, 32, 36, 45, 46, 47
signals, 43
silicon, 3, 23, 26, 29
simulation(s), 4, 5, 11, 12, 15, 17, 18, 19, 20, 21, 22, 24, 25, 26, 28, 29
single chain, 9
SNP, 37, 45
social security, x, 68
software, viii, 32, 42, 44, 51, 53, 54, 57, 60, 61, 62, 68
solution, 10, 72
spatial information, 57
species, viii, 8, 14, 22, 32, 36, 37, 40, 45, 47
sperm, 27

Index

stakeholders, x, 67
state, 10
statistics, viii, 31, 33, 44, 53
storage, ix, 7, 51, 53, 54, 61, 67
stress, viii, 32
structural modifications, 11
structure, 4, 5, 7, 8, 11, 15, 17, 26, 27, 29, 38, 50, 51, 54
substrate, 47
supervision, ix, 49
survival, vii, 2, 3

T

target, vii, 1, 3, 4, 15, 17, 40, 42
teachers, ix, 67, 70
techniques, 3, 10, 27, 33, 43, 57
technology(s), vii, viii, ix, 23, 31, 34, 36, 38, 45, 57, 61, 62, 64, 67, 69, 70
testing, 36, 37, 64
text mining, 40
theft, 70, 73
thymine, 5
time frame, 3
tissue, 2, 3, 4, 13, 17, 26, 28, 29
topology, 53
toxicology, 46
tracks, 3, 11, 12, 20, 22, 24, 28
traits, 36, 37
trajectory, 15
transcription, viii, 32, 41
transformation, 47, 51
transmission, 7
transport, 11, 28, 38
treatment, 2, 3, 15, 23, 37, 40
triggers, 8
tryptophan, 7

U

underlying mechanisms, 10

uniform, 21, 42
United Kingdom, 1, 65
universities, 64, 70
updating, 51
urban, 64

V

validation, vii, x, 25, 68
vandalism, 70
variables, 26, 33, 42, 43
variations, viii, 32
vector, 53, 57, 59
vegetation, 62, 63
victims, 70, 73
visualization, 33

W

waste, 8
water, 4, 8, 12, 13, 14, 15, 18, 21, 24, 26, 28, 29, 50, 54
wealth, 35, 38, 69
web, vii, ix, 46, 49, 50, 51, 53, 54, 57, 58, 59, 61, 62, 64, 70, 73
web browser, 59
web service, ix, 49, 50, 58, 59, 61, 73
workflow, 59, 60, 68
workforce, 68
worldwide, 61, 70
WWW, 62

X

XPS, 10

Y

yield, 17, 42

OCT 2013

QA 76.9 .A25 D352 2013

Data security, data mining, and data management :

WITHDRAWN

Middlesex County College
Library
Edison, NJ 08818